D1571992

PLATFORM

P R E S S

BUCKS COUNTY
PENNSYLVANIA

INSIDE THE
INFRASTRUCTURE
REVOLUTION

A ROADMAP FOR
REBUILDING AMERICA

MARY SCOTT NABERS
author of COLLABORATION NATION

Published in the United States by
Platform Press
The nonfiction imprint of
Winans Kuenstler Publishing, LLC
Doylestown, Pennsylvania 18901 USA
www.wkpublishing.com

Platform Press and colophon
are registered trademarks

First Edition

*This book is dedicated to
my business partners, clients, public sector friends,
and the visionary association and
industry leaders who have inspired me…
and to my living, supportive and wonderful family.*

Acknowledgments

The best ideas, insights, and examples chosen to appear here are the distillation of the past five years of conversations I've had with hundreds of clients, experts, colleagues, and advisors; from the many debates I witnessed or participated in; and from intensive research to establish the facts and interpret the results.

Ideas were exchanged over meals, with seat-mates on long flights, and in conversations in hallways at conferences with public officials who are veterans of large collaborative initiatives; infrastructure investors; and leaders in the business community of global contractors with established records of success in the designing, building, financing, operating, and maintenance of some of the signature public infrastructure projects of our time.

Special thanks are due the following—friends and colleagues who took time to help enrich the usefulness of this book.

- Martin Klepper, Ex. Dir., US Dept. of Transportation's Build American Bureau;
- Michael Dean, Ex. Dir., National Assoc. of Water Companies;
- The Honorable Henry Cisneros, Principal of Siebert, Cisneros, Shank & Co., and Co-Chair of the of the Bipartisan Policy Center Housing Commission;
- Michael Likosky, Head of Infrastructure Practice, 32 Advisors;
- Doug Peterson, CEO of S&P Global and Co-Chair of the Bipartisan Policy Center CEO Council on Infrastructure;
- John Parkinson, Ex. Dir., Assoc. for the Improvement of American Infrastructure (AIAI);
- Lisa Buglione, Director of Operations, Assoc. for the Improvement of American Infrastructure (AIAI);
- Larry Casey, Senior VP-Marketing, Skanska AB;
- Joe Wingerter, VP/Development, Kiewit Corporation;
- Marcus J. Lemon, Chairman-Infrastructure & Public-Private Partnerships Group, Polsinelli LLP

- Patrick Rhode, VP/Corporate Affairs, Cintra, S.A.;
- Chancellor John Sharp, Texas A&M University;
- Todd Herberghs, Ex. Dir., National Council of Public Private Partnerships (NCPPP);
- Diane Barrett, Special Assistant, Office of the Mayor, City and County of Denver;
- Kelly Leid, former Ex. Dir. of the Mayor's Office of the National Western Center, City & County of Denver;
- Lyndon Dacuan, Content/Communications Mgr, Onvia Inc.;
- Paul Irby, Analytics & Strategy Consultant, Onvia Inc.;
- Richard Timbs, Senior Director, Global Infrastructure Hub, University of Sydney, Australia;
- Dr. John Brown Miller, Founder/President, Ironsides Strategies;
- Marshall Macomber, President, Think P3, LLC;
- Frank Rapoport, Chief Strategy Advisor, Assoc. for the Improvement of American Infrastructure (AIAI);
- Andrew Schendle, Dir. of Business Development, AECOM
- Rodney Moss, Sr VP , Hunt Companies;
- Ken Bloom, Sr. Client Partner, Global Transportation and Logistics Services, Korn Ferry;
- Lisa Washington, Director of Client Relations , IP3
- Jennifer Hare, P3 Services, TetraTech/Institute for P3s;
- Phillip Ray, Vice Chancellor, Texas A&M University;
- Mark Romoff, Pres./CEO, Canadian Council for PPP;
- The Strategic Partnerships Team: Gay Erwin; Tommy Huntress; John Breier; Roy Hogan; Kirk Yoshida; Edgar Antu; Laura Matisi; Colby Harrell; Anne Marie Willsey; Turner Kimbrough; Paula Morelock; Kristin Gordon; Beth Corbett; Ben Nakhaima; Brittany Gaddy; Bryn Terry; Maya Ingram; Rich Stella; Talan Tyminski; Haley Dearing; John Barton; Jeanine Finn; and Joshua Emeneger.

Contents

Digest

My dad, mayor of our hometown, owned a small West Texas newspaper for 30 years. This quote, one of my favorites, appeared below the masthead on every edition. It is a wise reminder of purpose—the greater good—for all who are committed to rebuilding America.

For when the One Great Scorer comes
To mark against your name,
He marks — not that you won or lost —
*But how you played the Game.**

*From the poem "Alumnus Football" by sportswriter Grantland Rice (1880-1954).

About the Author

Mary Scott Nabers is president and CEO of Strategic Partnerships, Inc. (SPI), an Austin, Texas-based consulting firm that has been facilitating partnerships between public officials and the private sector since 1995, drawing on the knowledge and experience of its team of experts in government affairs, business development, procurement consulting, and communications.

She served from 1992 to 1994 as a Texas State Railroad Commissioner, overseeing an agency that regulated the state's $65 billion energy and transportation complexes. Before that she served for eight years as the commissioner representing the business community on the Texas Employment Commission where she founded the Texas Business Council. She earned her MBA from the University of Texas at Austin.

During her decade in state government, Nabers wrote a weekly syndicated newspaper column, hosted a weekly radio program, and published a monthly business magaine with a circulation of 160,000. She currently publishes *Texas Government Insider* and a national publication, *Government Contracting Pipeline*.

Nabers has represented Texas on the National Petroleum Council, the National Coal Council, and the Interstate Oil and Gas Compact, among other organizations She has been a regular speaker at government and industry events for the past 25 years.

Her first book, *Collaboration Nation*, published in 2012, introduced readers to the developing market for infrastructure joint ventures. *Inside The Infrastructure Revolution* explores how these joint ventures, called public-private partnerships, have evolved into increasingly sophisticated vehicles for improving our public services and rebuilding the public assets that are essential to our nation's prosperity.

 Preface

In the six years since the publication of my first book, *Collaboration Nation*, I have been invited to speak to dozens of audiences across the country about the essential role of private capital in fixing our worn-out civil infrastructure.

To the executives of companies that have solutions to offer, I explain the inner workings of government procurement and the basics of procurement contracts.

To groups of public officials, I explain the benefits of creating infrastructure joint ventures with the private sector—commonly known as public-private partnerships. They make it possible to accelerate infrastructure projects while reducing the risk to taxpayers of unexpected costs, delays, and disputes.

The top three questions raised by public officials are:

- What is a public-private partnership (a PPP or P3)?
- Where does the money come from?
- Are public-private partnerships harmful to taxpayers?

The detailed answers to all three will be found on the following pages, but I offer a simple metaphor to keep in mind as you read—how you finance the purchase of a home.

What does it really cost to own a home? For the purposes of this illustration, assume the purchase price is financed by a thirty-year mortgage, you intend to live in it for the full term (e.g., not an investment), and there are no real estate taxes to pay and no income tax deductions to take.

An existing home may need alterations and upgrades on day one to make it fully functional, or to suit your needs. Even if it is a new house, you'll have thirty years of weather, wear and tear, and natural decay, all of which will take a toll on the structure and essential systems. The grounds need to be maintained—there's grass to cut, snow to plow, trees to trim, etc.

On top of all those expenses, you'll be paying premiums for your homeowner's insurance policy. The Federal Reserve Board estimates that, on average, homeowner insurance costs $3.50 a year per $1,000 of purchase price, so our $300,000 home costs $1,050 a year to insure. Estimates of the annual cost to maintain a newly built $300,000 house average out to about $2,500 a year over time.

At the end of a thirty-year mortgage at current rates, the actual cost of the house—purchase price, interest, maintenance, and insurance—comes to nearly $700,000.

Now imagine that the bank offers you the option to include in your mortgage payment all those other expenses. If the roof ever needs repairing, the bank will pay for it. If termites infest your garage, the bank will have them exterminated and the damage repaired. If the heat pump dies, the bank will replace it. If the driveway pavement buckles, the bank will have it fixed. The bank will pay to keep the grass mowed, the pool cleaned, and the leaves raked.

Furthermore, the bank guarantees that at the end of the thirty years—when the last mortgage payment has been made and you own the house free and clear—it will be in good repair. Finally, assume the contract has a provision that if the bank fails to keep its promises, you can fire the bank and find a new one to take over the contract and fix whatever needs repairing, at no additional cost to you.

Your choice then would be between making just the mortgage payments and hoping you'll have the cash you'll need when major repairs pop up, or making a slightly higher monthly payment and having all the costs and risks of upkeep become the bank's responsibility.

That, roughly speaking, is the outline of a typical public-private partnership.

It sounds simple and, in theory, it is. In this book I have tried to touch on a few of the many permutations and applications, as well as the benefits and pitfalls, as part of the larger conversation we need to have about how to rebuild our way out of America's infrastructure crisis. We are in urgent need of solutions and the only way the US will stay competitive in a global economy is by creating collaborations that tap into the best practices of both the public and private sectors.

The answer to the last question I'm so often asked? No, public-private partnerships are not harmful to taxpayers. However, doing nothing will be.

—Mary Scott Nabers

# 1 Infrastructure Crisis Defined

C risis is the mother of most revolutions, and the decline in America's infrastructure is developing into the biggest crisis we've faced since the economic collapse of 2008. It's the cumulative effect of a series of alarming regional crises that have been occurring with increased frequency and scope, from coast to coast and border to border. In the past dozen years, especially since the bellwether collapse of the Interstate 35 bridge in Minneapolis in 2007, flaws and failures in America's civil infrastructure have been afflicting ever-larger populations with ever-worsening consequences.

If you are a public official, this is not news. For most Americans, however, the extent of the problem is what they see on the streets of their communities through the windows of the cars, buses, and trains that get them to and from their jobs, errands, and family outings. To grasp the magnitude of what is happening, it's worth reviewing some of the signature events that have affected large numbers of people and become part of our country's shared narrative.

After the I-35 bridge collapse, engineers inspected and

documented about 50,000 bridges in the US that former Transportation Secretary Ray LaHood described as "dangerous," including one in five of the 4,000 spans that keep the river city of Pittsburgh humming. Among those 50,000 are failures just waiting to happen or safety-driven closures that are already disrupting commerce and interfering with public access to essential services.

As this book goes to press, New York City—the world's financial capital and the nation's business hub—is engaged in a chronic struggle with near-daily breakdowns in its aging public transit system. The wider metro area is dealing with a bottleneck caused by a cross-Hudson rail tunnel that was designed and built for the world as it existed in the age of steam, 1900, when the region's population was a quarter of what it is today.

No problem has affected more people more profoundly than water.

No infrastructure problem has affected people more profoundly than water. In 2005, Hurricane Katrina overwhelmed New Orleans' levee system, later found to have been inadequately designed, built, and maintained. In 2012, Hurricane Sandy flooded New York City's electrical substations, part of a century-old system; left eight million metro-area residents in the dark for days; and damaged a crucial Northeast Corridor rail link.

Hurricane Harvey drowned Houston in 2017 because of an inadequate flood-control system that relied on two dams that were built just after World War II, when the population was a tenth of what it is today. Just weeks later, Hurricane Irma destroyed nearly all of Puerto Rico's outdated electric grid, leaving many of the island's 3.4 million residents in the dark for months.

A recent five-year drought in California became a major crisis for 40 million residents because the region's reservoirs—most built before 1970—were designed to address floods, not droughts, for half as many people. We learned in recent years that thousands of Flint, Michigan, residents were exposed to toxic levels of lead that was leaching from old pipes into the water supply. Experts tell us to expect many more such water utility failures in the years ahead.

Transportation and water are big issues but they represent a fraction of the country's infrastructure needs. A 2016 report by the Reason Foundation, a libertarian think tank, listed a broad range of public services and facilities needing modernization:

- 130 large, medium and small hub airports
- 44,000 miles of non-tolled highways nearing or exceeding their fifty-year design lives
- Over 2,000 municipal electric and gas utilities
- 99 seaports
- 56,000 municipal water systems
- 15,000 wastewater treatment facilities

The Tipping Point

From my vantage point—as a former government official and, for the past two decades, as a consultant to government contractors—I am convinced that we've reached the tipping point. How we address our infrastructure issues and how we find the political consensus and the trillions of dollars needed will shape our economy in the near term and may well define the nation's future at home and on the world stage.

We know this much: There will be no quick or comprehensive federal fix. The previous administration learned that lesson the hard way with its 2009 American Recovery and Reinvestment Act, a $787 billion appropriation that was supposed to jump-start a cornucopia of "shovel-ready" projects across the country. The enabling legislation that Congress ultimately passed allocated less than $100 billion for transportation and infrastructure. The Congressional Budget Office later estimated that only $27.5 billion of that was actually spent on highways and bridges.

President Obama later told the *New York Times* that he learned, "There's no such thing as shovel-ready projects."

Even if it turns out there is support for a marquee federal infrastructure appropriation, it first has to make up for a decline of nearly 10 percent in federal infrastructure spending over the past decade. The current administration has signaled it isn't interested in underwriting local infrastructure projects.

In the fact sheet for its proposed 2018 budget, the White House noted, "The flexibility to use federal dollars to pay for essentially local infrastructure projects has created an unhealthy dynamic in which state and local governments delay projects in the hope of receiving Federal funds."

Revolutions develop from the ground up and in this case the ground is in the cities, counties, and states where the need is most apparent and urgent, and where waiting for federal help is no longer an option. Innovative projects are being launched across the country, driven by financing mechanisms that are common in many other countries but are only now being embraced in the US—private investment in the development and maintenance of public assets, and in the delivery of public services.

Revolutions develop from the ground up, in this case in the cities, counties, and states where the need is most apparent and urgent.

These types of projects were the subject of my first book, *Collaboration Nation*, published in 2012 in the aftermath of the Great Recession. At that time, public agencies at every jurisdictional level were starving for the funds and resources required to provide essential services, let alone deal with long-term infrastructure issues. Hardly a week went by that a government entity somewhere wasn't proposing privatizing some public obligation. Because private investment in public projects in the US was an unfamiliar tactic, the most common collaboration between public and private partners was privatization of various types of services. The results of that strategy were at best mixed.

The Philadelphia Gas Works Failure

For example, when my first book appeared in 2012, the city of Philadelphia, hoping to raise money to plug a yawning gap in the city's pension fund, was beginning the process of trying to sell its financially ailing energy utility, Philadelphia Gas Works, to a private company. Interest was high, attracting more than thirty bidders for an asset valued at roughly $2 billion. Two years later, pushback by the union representing the utility's 1,400 workers had been so effective that not a single member of the city council would support the deal that was negotiated, at a cost of more than $20 million in legal and other fees. Today the Philadelphia Gas Works' financial condition is no better.

At the same time, a number of cities were trying to raise cash by leasing public parking facilities. In Chicago, the downside of inexperience and a poorly vetted privatization became clear when the city's decision to lease its 36,000 meters to an investment group turned into a financial and political controversy. The city received an up-front payment of about $1.2 billion in exchange for a seventy-five-year lease with an operating company that would maintain the meters and repay investors out of revenue. The deal appealed to city officials because it effectively moved public employees and their pension obligations off the city's books and gave Chicago a rainy-day fund, which it promptly used to reduce budget deficits.

However, the contract included the requirement that the city reimburse the vendor for lost revenue due to street closings. In a major city like Chicago, parking spaces are frequently out of service—for parades, street fairs, marathons, road work, snow removal, etc. Every year, the lease has been a cash burden, costing the city about $9 million in 2015.

Before the credit crisis of 2008, state and local governments emboldened by surging tax revenue from the housing boom increased their outstanding debt obligations by about a third. Then the fading economy began to take its bite and by 2011 state and local budgets nationwide had racked up an estimated total shortfall of $3 trillion.

Six years after *Collaboration Nation* appeared we are all, public executives and private vendors alike, a lot smarter and wiser. We've learned about the risks of privatization—selling off public assets and monetizing future revenue. We've had to face the fact that the traditional model in which government acts as general contractor to build a new stretch of highway or a school, financing it through municipal bonds or other public finance vehicles, can be equally risky. When public entities become general contractors and something goes wrong, governments and taxpayers are ultimately on the hook.

It was clear six years ago that we had no choice but to reinvent how the people's business gets done, and it's even clearer today. Many state governments are still trying to recover from cuts made in federal spending during the recession. The National Association of State Budget Officers, a nonpartisan research group, projects that this fiscal year, 2018, almost half the states will end up in the red. Sufficient public funding to fix our infrastructure problems isn't there.

"This isn't simply a matter of 'we're running short this year,'" Traci Gleason, a spokeswoman with the Missouri Budget Project told the PBS program *NewsHour*. "We have made a series of policy decisions over the past several decades that starved our state of the services that were needed to grow our economy and create good quality jobs."

The needs as well as -he opportunities are enormous. Much of America's electric transmission and distribution system, projected to last fifty years, was constructed in the 1950s and 1960s.

Nearly 650,000 miles of high-voltage power systems are operating at full capacity and cannot accommodate future growth.

The US has nearly 15,000 wastewater treatment plants that are projected to acquire an additional 56 million new customers over the next twenty years. The estimate of the capital needed to meet that demand approaches $300 billion.

"We have starved the services that can grow our economy and create good-quality jobs."

The American Society of Civil Engineers (ASCE), which has issued an annual report card on the state of America's infrastructure since the 1980s, has estimated that by 2025 the US will be facing an infrastructure gap of almost $1.5 trillion. The US Department of Transportation has estimated that shoring up the nation's roads and bridges will cost more than $800 billion.

The goal of my first book was to draw attention to the problem and encourage forward-looking, evidence-based approaches. Since then, we've learned that privatizations of public assets are short-term fixes. We've learned that government will be unable to underwrite even a majority of our most pressing infrastructure needs. But since 2012, we've also seen many successful infrastructure projects completed and the evidence is inarguably positive. My goal in this book is to explore new approaches, the use of alternative funding through public private partnerships, demystify how they work, and provide a roadmap for growing our way back to full strength.

The Politics of Private Investment

Why private investment in public infrastructure makes sense, and why it has become so widely used abroad, boils down to two principal elements both partners make: 1) long-term commitments; and 2) agree to sharing the risk. Projects that are well planned, intelligently designed, and transparently negotiated will almost always guarantee mutually assured success.

Politically, however, the role of the private sector remains a tough sell in many US jurisdictions, in part because of the widely reported problems cited earlier. Political optics can distort good, practical ideas and interfere with common sense. Even in states that are considered the most business-friendly, elected officials tell me they worry about giving their opponent's campaign ammo if they propose collaborative projects that could be misrepresented in ads to sound like government giveaways.

The other impediment to the full flowering of public-private partnerships has, until recently, been America's "liquid and robust tax-exempt debt market, which has financed trillions of dollars of infrastructure at very low cost," writes Sarah Kline, a research fellow with the Bipartisan Policy Council, a public policy think tank. "Tax-exempt debt has been so widely available, in fact, that for many years it virtually eliminated any incentive for state and local governments to explore other options for delivering infrastructure."

Recession and federal cutbacks made states and cities wary about taking on new debt.

For this and other reasons, there is growing interest in modifying or eliminating the sacred cow of tax-exempt municipal bonds. It's unlikely there will be any significant changes in the short term. Either way, in spite of the urgency of decrepit bridges, contaminated water, and a myriad of other infrastructure needs, the Great Recession and cutbacks in federal subsidies have made all public agencies wary about taking on new debt.

In the gap between need and capacity is where the infrastructure revolution has begun. It has the potential to become a boon for the private sector while producing a bonanza of innovative, effective, and efficient solutions for infrastructure problems that would otherwise have languished for years, sapping our nation's productivity and limiting our prosperity.

The challenge for business will be increased competition and expectations. The challenge for government officials and executives will be to learn how to build support for collaboration in their communities from the ground up, where all successful revolutions begin.

2 Mars, Venus and Cupid

I n his 1992 best-selling book *Men Are From Mars, Women Are From Venus*, relationship counselor John Gray employed a clever metaphor to provoke a discussion about the different ways men and women respond to stress. He said couples going through rough patches can build healthier relationships by first acknowledging and accepting those intrinsic gender-specific differences.

The same might be said about the relationship between business and government when it comes to collaborating on public projects. Success in business requires a competitive, action-oriented approach to solving problems, overcoming obstacles, and seizing opportunities. Profit is the principal measure of progress.

Success in government calls for a reflective, process-oriented approach—public officials are accustomed to moving slowly and studying all the options. It takes skill to find consensus amid the push and pull of competing constituencies. Those who make a career of government typically have a deep emotional commitment to helping others and contributing to the greater good. Their role models range from Thomas Jefferson ("The care of human life and happiness is the first and only legitimate objective of good government.") to John F. Kennedy ("Ask what you can do for your country.").

You might say that business leaders are from Mars and public officials are from Venus. I'm from both. By the time I graduated from high school, my father—the mayor of our small West Texas town and publisher of the local newspaper—had inspired me to see public service as noble and capitalism as exciting. At the age of sixteen I started the first of many small businesses that helped pay my way through college and graduate school.

My late husband, Lynn, became a long-serving state legislator while I built a small media company—two radio stations and a newspaper. From my bully pulpit I wrote and spoke out about exasperating experiences I'd experienced in dealing with government agencies. In those days I was definitely from Mars.

After I sold the media company, I had the chance to put my ideas into action when I was appointed by the governor to serve on the Texas Employment Commission (now the Texas Workforce Commission). My responsibilities included representing the interests of the state's 380,000 employers. For eight years I was an outspoken advocate for making government more responsive, helping entrepreneurs grow their ventures and create jobs by making compliance less onerous, costly, and time consuming.

I spent many days traveling the state, listening to employers, offering advice, finding resources, answering questions, and handing out literature. I encouraged my colleagues in government to focus on building trusting relationships between business and government, to look for opportunities for collaborations instead of confrontations, to emphasize solutions over sanctions.

My last two years in public service were as a member of the Texas Railroad Commission, at that time the state's most powerful, complex, and political regulatory agency. Our rulings affected $65 billion of the state's annual economy, principally the energy and transportation sectors. It was an enormous tangle of state and federal regulations with high stakes on all sides.

By the time I left, I knew exactly what it's like to be from Venus.

Since that time, I have played a third metaphorical role, as intermediary between the two—a sort of Cupid. For more than two decades I have been the CEO of Strategic Partnerships, Inc., a business development firm whose consultants help broker joint ventures between the public and private sectors. We guide corporate clients through the thickets and labyrinths of state and local procurement cultures and processes. From time to time I have also helped government executives navigate the swift currents and sharp elbows of the business world.

In this book, I hope Mars will meet Venus and Venus will learn to understand Mars. We have a lot in common, a solid base to build on.

Although we have shepherded many successful and profitable relationships, matchmaking is rarely easy. In recent years it has become more complex and fast-moving: innovations made possible by technology; new financial products and techniques; more astute and aggressive competition among vendors; leaner public budgets; and the increasingly shrill tone in our public discourse that drowns out too many good ideas. Yet good ideas, like weeds heroically sprouting through pavement, still manage to take root and flourish.

Reinventing The Electric Grid

One area worth noting is the generation and distribution of electric power. Some visionaries, through collaboration, are reimagining and reshaping the nation's electric grid. New York, home to the nation's oldest power system and some of the worst blackouts, is emerging as one of the states leading the way.

Of its 20 million residents, nearly 13 million—more than 60 percent—live in or around New York City, within striking distance of major ocean-driven weather events. Every year there are nor'easters, ice storms, blizzards, or hurricanes that bring down miles of transmission lines and damage other elements of the region's grid. In 2012, Hurricane Sandy set a record when it caused flooding that destroyed the Lower Manhattan generators that power the world's most active securities exchanges and shut down the subway system, the city workforce's lifeline.

Long Islanders suffered the worst and longest-lasting outages. After the clouds had parted and the system was up and running again, New York's Governor Mario Cuomo declared the Long Island Power Authority "broken." After years of complaints about poor customer service and high rates, "It is the status quo and it's failed." Under an operating agreement, the Long Island system was taken over by PSEG, a publicly traded company with a long history and deep roots in bordering New Jersey.

The good idea that came out of it all was not handed down from the top. It bubbled up from the hardest-hit towns. Residents were appalled when the new operator replaced thousands of standard-sized poles with new ones that were eighty feet tall, towering over the stately old shade trees and Cape Cod cottages that line their streets.

The complaints coincided with surging interest in micro-grids, small energy systems designed to generate enough power to maintain stable service within a defined boundary. Today, the state has more than 200 micro-grids in operation, from those able to power one city block up to large remote hydro systems.

Good ideas abound. For example, we're reimagining and reshaping the nation's electric grid.

This corner of the infrastructure revolution is just beginning to percolate. Connecticut's Wesleyan University has built its own micro-grid. Plans are being drawn up for a grid to protect New York City's food distribution center. California power suppliers are looking at micro-grids as a way to help them meet state requirements for increasing renewable energy sources.

Micro-grids have become viable because of lower-cost, advanced technologies like wind, solar, and tidal generation that bring power sources closer to users. Improved battery storage is making micro-grids reliable backups and even replacements for dependence on large sprawling networks where regional power outages indiscriminately disrupt service.

The good idea was not handed down from the top but bubbled up from the hardest-hit towns.

If you are a current or aspiring vendor or investor—from Mars—infrastructure is a huge growth market waiting for good ideas and efficient delivery. Demonstrated successes can be leveraged by replication across multiple markets. If you are a government official or agency executive—from Venus—public support for innovative solutions is growing.

"Transportation ballot measures have become an enormous success story … with up to three quarters of transit-focused measures passing in recent years," according to a recent Brookings Institution report. As a result of the November 2016 election, "Billions of dollars in additional infrastructure investment are coming in the form of newly approved bonds, taxes, and other sources of revenue."

For all those billions, however, the amount of funding needed to repair, replace, and upgrade public transportation assets, plus build the new infrastructure we'll require for the next 50 to 100 years, is staggering. We've fallen so far behind in deferred maintenance and delayed upgrades and expansions that public funding will never be enough to allow us to catch up.

The only option, the one that brings Mars and Venus together in a mutually supportive collaboration, will be the third way, private investment in public assets. We have ample evidence that the third way works because it's been the predominant financing mechanism for years in countries such as Canada, Australia, India, Japan, and the UK. The roadmap for rebuilding America exists. We just need to follow it.

3 The Four Paradoxes

We may be a divided nation on many important issues, but we agree by a wide margin that the US urgently needs an infrastructure makeover. When the current administration came out of the gate naming as one of its top priorities a $1 trillion public works initiative, three out of four adults told a Gallup poll that they supported it.

Among the multiple paradoxes embedded in this discussion is the disconnect between users and payers. While support for infrastructure spending has grown across the political spectrum, government spending on public works has been shrinking. Census Bureau data for the second quarter of 2017 showed infrastructure spending as a percent of the country's economic output fell to 1.4 percent, a record low. In thirty-four states, inflation-adjusted government spending on construction projects was lower in 2016 than it had been a decade earlier.

America's public infrastructure, essential to our prosperity and security, is wearing out even as governments at all levels have had to tighten spending to reflect the political climate. Some states are raising fuel taxes to address road and bridge repairs. New Jersey's gas tax went from lowest in the country to highest, although getting it passed by the legislature required a flurry of offsetting tax cuts that will dampen the net benefit to highways.

The Disconnect Between Users and Payers

That brings us to the second paradox. In most jurisdictions, there is immediate and stiff opposition to raising taxes and user fees to finance repairs or upgrades to water, sewer, power, and the other essential civil and quasi-government services. Yet voters have been consistently approving new bond issues for public works, ignoring the fact that debt service ultimately comes out of the same public purse.

The third and most frustrating paradox is that we don't have to depend on the public purse. Wall Street has identified infrastructure as a large, attractive, and growing market worldwide, and is eager to provide the expertise and resources to rebuild America. In May 2017, Blackstone Group, one of the largest investment firms in the world, launched an infrastructure fund, saying it ultimately expects to invest more than $100 billion in public infrastructure projects. According to some observers, the vast majority of that will be invested based on the current administration's plans for related tax credits for pipelines, storage terminals, cargo facilities, power utilities, and other commercial assets with long-term revenue streams.

The fourth and final paradox is that the financial solution—involving private capital—is relatively simple and it's been around since the country was founded. America has a history of private sector investment in public projects and public-private partnerships are routine in many other countries. Yet some groups perceive the private sector's interest in

Infrastructure is a huge growth market waiting for good ideas and efficient delivery.

the public arena as a kind of financial chicanery cooked up on Wall Street—a giveaway, handing over control of public assets to private companies that use them for profit. That's not only a profound misunderstanding, it also fails to acknowledge the long and storied role of collaborative projects in our history.

When done well, collaborative partnerships with alternative types of financing not only allow critical projects to be launched, they shift risk from the public to the private sector; increase the availability and quality of public services; and bolster government balance sheets and cash flow. Some of the most effective collaborations have been based on the simplest concepts.

For example, at the start of the Revolutionary War, America's navy consisted of a handful of ships commissioned by the colonies and crewed by volunteers. To bulk up, the Continental Congress issued licenses to entrepreneurs willing to operate armed ships and attack British merchant vessels in exchange for the lion's share of the money and goods they recovered. Those privateers took all the risk of losing their ships, being captured, or being killed. In the end, they were so successful at intercepting British vessels and capturing cargoes that historians consider the campaign a deciding factor in the war's outcome as well as a crucial source of investment capital for the newly formed nation.

Our modern system of super highways has its roots in the 1790s with the privately financed Philadelphia and Lancaster Turnpike, predecessor of today's Pennsylvania Turnpike. All of America's railroads were built with private capital.

One of the most significant collaborations in American history was launched in 1843 when Congress voted to underwrite the $30,000 cost of Samuel Morse's first experimental telegraph line from Baltimore to Washington. The telegraph was as revolutionary in its day as was the Internet—which evolved out of a taxpayer-funded Department of Defense program—150 years later. Each was a powerful engine of economic growth.

Until the 1930s, city transit systems and electricity grids

were operated primarily by private companies under exclusive government franchises. The Great Depression drove many of those privately owned, essential public service companies into bankruptcy and they were taken over by government agencies. At the same time, President Franklin Roosevelt's New Deal programs created thousands of jobs with mega-projects like the Tennessee Valley Authority and the national electrical grid, considered two of the most successful financial public-private collaborations in US history.

Government Can Be The Solution

World War II sealed government's role as lead provider of public services, a role that manifested itself in every corner of the country beginning in the 1950s with the buildout of the toll-free interstate highway system. Postwar government at every level expanded in size, influence, and control.

Opinion began to shift in the 1980s when, during another financial crisis, President Ronald Reagan declared, "Government is not the solution to our problems; government IS the problem." We are still living today with a portrayal of government as the enemy of prosperity, a political climate that is anything but collaborative. Government and business operate in different worlds, but it's a fundamental mistake to think of them as combatants.

Signs of innovation first appeared in the early 1990s. Congress enacted the Intermodal Surface Transportation Efficiency Act (ISTEA), providing a way to combine federal, state, local, private, and toll funding for improving and expanding highway infrastructure. Meanwhile, contracting and ethics rules that had long prohibited architects from providing construction services were relaxed, clearing the way for more "design-build" projects, where a general contractor is selected to oversee all subcontractors for the design and construction of a facility, a more efficient system.

The emerging model today, "design-build-finance-operate-maintain," has added the element that helps clinch the argument for financing our infrastructure needs—a long-term commitment by investors and private contractors that is aligned

The new model aligns investors and contractors with the public. with the long-term goals of the public. Any contracting group whose income and profit are tied to a twenty-, thirty-, or 50-year operations and maintenance obligation will make sure the bridge, airport, or sewer treatment plant is designed and built to last.

Furthermore, governance and ownership of these assets always remains with the public. Taxpayers are the ultimate winners, a fact that is often overlooked. The public entity also sets the standards that must be met for operational quality and maintenance.

Public-Private Creativity

Under the traditional system, a contractor builds the asset and hands off operation and maintenance to others. With no ongoing responsibility, a contractor may cut corners and use cheaper materials. Instead of being responsible for decades of maintenance, operation, and availability, when the ribbon is cut the government is left on its own to deal with problems that may crop up in the future. All risk is on taxpayers.

Budget crunches and a weak public finance market have been catalysts for innovation. Today all sorts of creative collaborations are changing the way government provides services. For the first time in 125 years, a major highway link in New York City—the Goethals Toll Bridge between Staten Island and New Jersey—is being replaced with a new bridge financed, built, and to be maintained by a private sector firm. The money to repay investors and to fund maintenance costs will come from toll revenue over thirty years. The project was the first time a major New York infrastructure project was funded this way since the Brooklyn Bridge, completed in 1883.

A Port Authority spokesman described it as, "buying a bridge ... and getting a guaranteed warranty on it."

By some estimates, New York State alone will need some $250 billion in infrastructure upgrades in the coming decade. Through a bi-state agency—the Port Authority of New York and New Jersey—the region has become a leader in rethinking and re-engineering how it builds, maintains, and operates its bridges, tunnels, inter-urban transit systems, harbor facilities, and airports.

One of its most visible infrastructure successes has been the replacement for the Tappan Zee Bridge over the Hudson River, an arterial link in a crucial ring road around the metropolitan region that is vital to the economy of the Northeast. The original bridge, completed in 1955, had become a maintenance nightmare and commuter headache. It was in such disrepair that fixing it was not a viable option. The replacement Mario Cuomo Bridge, named for the former governor, opened in 2017. The $4 billion project was completed ahead of schedule and is forecast to save the Port Authority about $100 million a year in maintenance costs—$3 billion in total.

The Authority scored another big win in 2017 with an agreement to upgrade one of the principal terminals at New York City's LaGuardia Airport, ranked by many travelers as one of the worst in the world. Delta Airlines agreed to invest $4 billion to upgrade its terminal. The Port Authority projects that by the time the overhaul is complete, about $12 billion will have been invested in "complicated transportation construction with risk borne by the private sector and not the public." LaGuardia Airport is a public asset that is being leveraged to maintain New York's role as the world's business center.

P3s Get Creative

There are many examples of successful public-private partnerships. Illinois has outsourced management of its state lottery system. West Virginia selected a private sector partner for its nearly bankrupt workers' compensation system. Arizona and Florida, among others, have established councils on efficient government that identify, implement, and/or manage collaborative projects to improve government activities.

Governments in the UK and Canada have been using new financing techniques regularly since the early 1990s. Use of them in the US has taken longer to catch on because in most jurisdictions enabling legislation had to be written and adopted. In some places, political opposition has been strong. To date, thirty-four states have laws on the books providing for infrastructure joint ventures.

An example of an early collaboration that was simple and successful was completed in 2001 in Washington, DC. The city got a much-needed new school building—the James F. Oyster Bilingual Elementary School—at no public cost in exchange for giving a developer the right to build an apartment house on adjacent city land that for years had been a vacant lot overgrown with weeds and trash. These types of engagements are often called "asset recycling" projects.

The neighborhood got a boost of pride in the new school. Parents wanted to move there so their children could attend. A plot of barren land that had attracted rats and encouraged drug dealing was turned into a modern apartment house that generated real estate taxes and put money in the pockets of local businesses and tradespeople. The stock of affordable housing improved and taxpayers were the ultimate winners.

Experts predict more collaborations like these as elected officials find dormant or under-utilized assets that may have been on the public ledgers for a century or more and can be leveraged to improve existing public services and fund other needs.

Across the country today, military installations that were established during and after World War II are being decommissioned and repurposed as housing, office, and manufacturing developments. Think tanks have been lobbying state legislatures to conduct comprehensive inventories of all public lands and buildings so they can be actively managed—leased, utilized, or divested and returned to the tax rolls.

As a nation we have been hobbled by our paradoxes.

As simple and logical as many of these projects are, as a nation we have been hobbled by our paradoxes. Engineer and historian Henry Petroski provides an eloquent warning about our dilemma in his widely praised 2016 book, *The Road Taken: The History and Future of America's Infrastructure.*

> *Whether we like it or not, infrastructure is steeped in politics … We vote for roads and against potholes; for fixing our bridges and against the taxes to do so; for pork and earmarks but not necessarily for the common good. … Our nation and its states are at a fork in the road today, and which path they choose … will make all the difference in whether our roads, highways, and bridges—and the economy that so relies on them—can truly be revitalized. It is imperative that we take into account the successes and, especially, the failures of the past in choosing the path to the future.*

4   The Three Ps

For the past two decades, the prevailing term for projects that involve private investment in public infrastructure has been public-private partnership—PPP or P3. In a world awash with acronyms, P3 has become the default shorthand to describe a variety of engagements that represent long-term infrastructure collaborations between the public and private sectors.

Today, in spite of the preponderance of successes over failures, the term public-private partnership has become fraught with political baggage that is getting in the way of intelligent, sensible solutions that lead to efficient delivery of public facilities and services. For that reason, many public officials and private contractors are avoiding the term. Those of us who are on the front lines of the infrastructure revolution may need to come up with a new lexicon that goes beyond acronyms. But first, it's helpful to know a little history.

The United Kingdom and Canada were early adopters of the concept of hybrid solutions and alternative funding options for the mismatch between growing populations and aging facilities. The granddaddy of public-private partnerships in the modern age is the Channel Tunnel (the "Chunnel"), now known as the Eurotunnel, the undersea rail line that connects England and France beneath the English Channel. The tunnel took eight years to build, opening in 1994 at a final inflation-adjusted cost of about $25 billion—twice the original estimate.

The project was financed by private debt and the sale of shares in a newly formed company that was to build and maintain it as part of a long-term management contract. A year after the Euro-

Think tanks have been lobbying state legislatures to take inventory of public lands and buildings so they can be actively managed and returned to the tax rolls.

tunnel opened, the company defaulted on its debt and was forced to reorganize. The project (first proposed in the early 19th century) was controversial—a diplomatic, economic, and political hot potato.

The Eurotunnel: A 5-for-1 Return

In spite of a tangle of financial, legal, and regulatory issues, the Eurotunnel has been a huge success. In a 2016 report, accounting firm Ernst & Young calculated that today the tunnel facilitates annual trade and tourism worth more than US $120 billion—almost $5 of economic activity for each dollar it cost to build. And it generates this kind of return to taxpayers every year.

The tunnel project taught some important lessons that demonstrated how these contracts and relationships should be structured. Those who become party to them should take the long view in planning and projection. The Eurotunnel stumbled initially because it began without a well-researched and coordinated master plan. No project so enormous, requiring multinational cooperation, had ever been attempted and it deserved more planning.

Today's collaborations are increasingly sophisticated and, unlike the Eurotunnel, most shift the risk of failure from government to private sector contractors but they must be planned carefully. Another lesson we should heed is that major projects like the tunnel may seem outrageously costly at the time but, short of a bridge-to-nowhere proposal, they are long-term investments that reward all parties, handsomely, in the form of increased economic prosperity and the maintenance of important public assets.

By the time the Eurotunnel opened in 1994, P3s had begun to appear elsewhere in the UK and in Canada. The Canadian government has embraced P3s since 1993 and, since 2009, has become a prominent facilitator of major projects through its P3 Canada Fund, governed by a federal agency—PPP Canada. PPP Canada bills itself as "a leading source of expertise on PPP matters … assessing and executing P3 opportunities." Canada is considered the most active P3 market in the world, and the most mature.

According to InfraAmericas, a corporate research group, federal and provincial governments have facilitated about 250 projects representing about $120 billion of private capital invested in hospitals, bridges, highways, rapid transit lines, water utilities, and sewage treatment systems. There have been no major failures in Canada and estimated savings from avoiding cost overruns are projected to be many billions. Still, private investment in public projects has been a topic of hot debate.

Opponents of P3s complain that the overall cost of most projects is higher than they theoretically would be if managed and funded by government using public debt. While it may be true that private companies will have somewhat higher financing costs and must factor some cost for the risks they are willing to incur, the argument that government can do it cheaper is undermined by history and experience. And, it is important to factor in the value of private sector expertise and experience as well as the ongoing maintenance and operational responsibilities that fall to the private sector partner. Those value propositions are extremely significant to governmental entities.

Today's infrastructure joint-venture contracts often include incentives for projects that are built on time and on budget, and penalties for those that aren't. Instead of cost overruns that land on the public balance sheet and cause political turmoil, the financial risk is borne entirely by the private sector. When construction of a large ring-road highway in Calgary ran late, the contractor had to pay a fine of $70,000 a day. It is hard to find any public officials who have been a part of a successful public-private partnership who are not eager to discuss the benefits of the engagement. And they are willing to share their advice and best practices with their counterparts in other locations.

The Net Economic Impact Factor

The process of putting together, evaluating, or scoring a proposed infrastructure venture should include an analysis of the net economic effect. It's a speculative exercise, but it is important and informative. In 2016, the nonpartisan, nonprofit Canadian Council for Public-Private Partnerships did some serious number crunching and analysis to help public officials measure in dollars and cents the return on investment from public-private partnerships.

Using a big-data approach, researchers reverse-engineered interactions among more than 40 million stakeholders—individuals, government, business, and nonprofits—across 5,500 jurisdictions. In the end, the council reported that every $1.00 invested in infrastructure added between $2.40 and $3.60 cents to the country's GDP. The best results were found in projects that bundled multiple related public services—a new hospital wing and housing for the elderly, for example.

Criticism of infrastructure joint ventures tends to be political or cultural in nature. Skeptics ask if it's right for private companies to use public assets for profit. Skeptics will question what happens in twenty, thirty, fifty years if the private sector partner falters on the contract. The more important question to ask, however, is how is it possible to address the country's crumbling infrastructure without private sector capital.

The Language and Definition of PPPs

The universe of stakeholders in infrastructure joint ventures may find a better term to replace public-private partnership, but the definition will still be nebulous. Academics have been pointing out with increasing frequency in recent years that there is no one description of a P3. There are many types of engagement models for public-private partnerships but they all have some common components.

On its website, this is how PPP Canada answers the question, "What is a P3?"

Public–Private Partnerships are a long-term performance-based approach to procuring public infrastructure where the private sector assumes a major share of the risks in terms of financing and construction and ensuring effective performance of the infrastructure, from design and planning, to long-term maintenance.

In practical terms, this means that:
- *Governments do not pay for the asset until it is built;*
- *A substantial portion of the cost is paid over the life of the asset and only if it is properly maintained and performs according to specifications; and*
- *The costs are known upfront and span the life-cycle*

of the asset, meaning that taxpayers are not on the financial hook for cost overruns, delays, or any performance issues over the asset's life.

P3s work because they engage the expertise and innovation of the private sector and the discipline and incentives of capital markets to deliver public infrastructure projects.

A shorter, more concise-sounding definition comes from two noted public policy experts and professors, David L. Weimer of University of Wisconsin, and Aidan R. Vining at Simon Fraser University in British Columbia.

A P3 typically involves a private entity financing, constructing, or managing a project in return for a promised stream of payments directly from government or indirectly from users over the projected life of the project or some other specified period of time.

The World Bank definition includes:

PPP project functions [that are] transferred to the private partner—such as design, construction, financing, operation, and maintenance—may vary from contract to contract, but the inclusion of privately raised finance is key to ensuring that the private partner is financially exposed and therefore incentivised to perform.

> *The argument that government can execute infrastructure projects cheaper than the private sector is undermined by history and experience.*

In the next chapter, I'll explain the details of different ways these projects can be structured. As for what to call them, "infrastructure joint venture" may be preferable. That term is increasingly being used to describe what we think of as public-private projects. A joint venture between a government entity and a private company is based on the same principles as one between two commercial partners:

> *An enterprise undertaken jointly by two or more parties in which they agree to pool their resources to accomplish a specific task while retaining their distinct identities.*

Perceptions matter in the public sphere and labels play a part in shaping public opinion. Whether we continue to call them P3s or some mash-up of infrastructure joint venture, history teaches us that what matters most in developing these projects are the agreements made before the first dollar is committed and the first spade of earth is turned. Great contracts and engagement agreements lead to successful projects. The reverse is equally true. Autopsies of failed projects usually find the root causes in ambiguous, poorly vetted, or open-ended contracts.

5 Obstacles and Opportunities

O utside of the infrastructure community there is a great deal of confusion and misapprehension about the role of business in public projects. There are also some unrealistic expectations about the role and capabilities of government. Public opinion surveys consistently find that a majority want government to do more with every kind of infrastructure—roads, airports, water supply, power, education, etc.

The problems are local—crumbling pavement, failing water mains, power interruptions—but surveys suggest respondents expect Congress to provide funding and solutions. Although infrastructure has been an on-again, off-again federal priority, the rhetoric has a wide swath of the public assuming that Uncle Sam is going to put up the money to fix everything that's broken.

Baked into the public's collective memory are some of the sweeping federal interventions of the past, like the New Deal and the War Production Board, infrastructure revolutions born of crises. More than eight decades after the Great Depression and World War II, and more than five decades after the buildout of the interstate grid, the federal role in building and maintaining infrastructure is a shadow of what it once was.

In the current climate it's impossible to imagine a scenario in which Congress would agree to a grand, expensive program that would result in upgrading local sewage treatment plants or replacing worn-out bridges, especially considering the amount of federal debt already outstanding.

All Infrastructure Is Local

Today's infrastructure revolution is a local problem because that's where the need is greatest. The Congressional Budget Office (CBO) calculates that state and local governments outspend the federal government by about three to one on transportation, drinking water, and wastewater infrastructure. Federal spending (about $100 billion) tends to be on structures and equipment whereas state and local infrastructure costs (about $300 billion) tend to be for operation and maintenance of public assets. That doesn't include the roughly $635 billion spent on public schools, of which 90 percent is paid for by state and local governments.

Local infrastructure is a trillion dollar marketplace, split along 50 states, 3,000 counties, 20,000 municipalities, plus thousands of public authorities, transportation agencies, universities, and quasi-public institutions.

The opportunities are abundant, but so are the obstacles. Infrastructure joint ventures are misunderstood and too often regarded by the public with distrust. There is always resistance to change and citizens always object to new or increased user fees.

Common Objections To Partnerships

The most common argument is, "We don't want private sector firms making profits from our public assets." Funding for repairs and expansion has to come from somewhere. It is the rare government agency that has surplus cash on hand.

Debt is the usual option, but many cities have had their bond ratings downgraded in recent years, making it more difficult and expensive to raise money.

Compared to Canada, the UK, and much of the rest of the world, the US has failed as a nation to engage the public in the debate and search for solutions to the infrastructure crisis. The market is so splintered and the subject so complex that it's been almost impossible to convey the message to a nation of 325 million people living in 20,000 towns that private capital is needed; that the bidding process is inherently transparent and competitive; that the process helps keep profit margins competitive, reasonable, and equitable; and that taxpayers will ultimately be the real winners.

The Unseen Benefit: Risk Transfer

Both the public and private sectors need to do a better job of explaining the economic value of shifting risk from taxpayers to investors. Public projects that are funded in the traditional way—with public funds and debt—rarely factor in maintenance and operational costs, expenses that creep up each year with inflation and never go away. Without adequate maintenance and operational investments, public assets deteriorate and quickly lose value.

In an infrastructure joint venture, maintenance and operational costs are part of the overall calculation from the start—design, build, finance, operate and maintain. Should costs exceed projections, the private sector partner—not the public agency—picks up the tab. These arrangements avoid the financial and political upheaval that often results when governments get hit with an unexpected bill and hard decisions have to be made about cutting other services or raising fees.

Another remark often heard in connection with infrastructure joint ventures is, "We already paid for those public assets. Why should we pay more?"

All assets, public and private, eventually require maintenance, repairs, improvements, and often expansion to accommodate demand. Buildings and equipment wear out. Technology becomes obsolete and equipment fails. One way or another, these bills come due. Without private partners, public agencies are on their own.

Those who complain about introducing or increasing highway tolls are unaware that the way joint ventures are structured, toll revenue underwrites the construction, maintenance, and repairs of free lanes.

Without a dedicated, full-court effort to develop public support for infrastructure collaborations, elected officials have no incentive to act and most will keep kicking the can down the road while the crisis deepens. Congress, under siege by vocal and organized opposition to private sector solutions, has resisted providing leadership, resources, regulatory reform, and incentives for joint venture projects.

Obstacles To Innovation

Existing regulatory processes and bureaucracy delay or kill many large projects. It can take years to complete required environmental studies and obtain approvals. Contractors can't wait that long. The most sought-after firms and their investors move on to more hospitable markets. Yet American elected officials will readily concede in private that it's just a matter of time before government has no other choice but to turn to the private sector to address the long list of infrastructure needs.

As a result, the US has been losing out on some cutting-edge approaches to providing public facilities and services.

Canada, with an economy and culture similar to ours, has learned how to message to citizens and taxpayers. It has provided structure for collaborative initiatives and is invested in ensuring that public-private partnerships are successful. Joint ventures now account for more than 20 percent of all infrastructure spending in Canada. It has become common there to see a headline like this one in 2017: "P3s, land sales help City of Saskatoon save $183 million in 2015."

After two decades of experience, Canadian taxpayers understand the benefits of collaboration so well that another article on the same page bore this startling headline: "Alberta government urged to explain why it rejects public-private partnerships."

Public support for joint ventures seems to be strong everywhere in the world but the US. In Asia, Europe, and Down Under, it is almost universally accepted that it is the best vehicle for financing infrastructure that encourages sustainable economic growth.

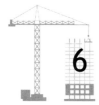

6 Capital, Capacity, Character

e're not in Canada, Europe, or Asia. We're in America, where infrastructure joint ventures have until recently been a work in progress while the rest of the world has been ironing out the kinks and fine-tuning the process. Whereas Canadians have had such a good experience that they press their public officials to enter into more partnerships, the US market—while overall successful—has sustained a few black eyes that critics cite to bolster their objections.

We've discussed a few examples of projects that ran off the rails, but it is important to look closer at these projects to assess the end result. What we find is that even projects that had difficulties left citizens and taxpayers whole, almost completely untouched, and always in possession of new and improved infrastructure assets.

There's hardly a jurisdiction in the country—maybe none—that hasn't, at one time or another, decided to take the plunge and build a new road maintenance barn, or a court-house, or extend a sewer line, and ended up suing one or more contractors. A roof leaks, the new high-tech building material was installed upside down, a trench crew with a backhoe severs the cables that run the city's emergency services network.

Nothing in life or infrastructure is smooth sailing from start to finish. Sometimes bad weather slows it down or blows the project off course. Sometimes it sinks the ship. Boston's Big Dig—a massive highway improvement project—is perhaps the most infamous example, giving public-private partnerships possibly their blackest eye.

The ambitious plan replaced a six-lane elevated central artery with an underground highway through downtown Boston, plus two bridges and other related improvements. It was such a massive, complex undertaking that *Insurance Journal*, an industry trade magazine, described it as "one of the biggest and most complex engineering undertakings in modern times." It earned the nickname "The Big Dig." The project's risk manager, Virginia Greiman, described it as larger than the Panama Canal and more expensive than the Eurotunnel.

Private capital invested in the public sector breaks the constant cycle of government having to do more with less.

The initial estimate given out publicly in the late 1980s was $2.4 billion, but engineers involved in the planning knew it would come in closer to $14 billion, according to Roger D. H. Warburton, a professor at Boston University's Metropolitan College. Warburton conducted an in-depth study of the Big Dig and discovered that the engineers on the project "warned everyone who would listen—including the politicians—that there were problems but no one wanted to heed their warnings."

The project generated the worst possible headlines and political fallout exacerbated by the discovery of serious construction flaws.

In spite of all the troubles surrounding the project and the company, all the partnership contracts were completed. As for the cost overruns and other problems, Professor Warburton calculates that annual cost savings to residents and businesses due to enhanced traffic flow are about $500 million a year. At that rate, the city of Boston has already benefitted by several billion dollars over and above what was paid to the private sector partner.

A P3 Success In Spite of Bankruptcy

In Texas, it was not faulty materials but inconvenient financial timing that brought down Ballenger Construction Co., a Texas-based contractor. According to legend, founder Joe Grover was twenty-four in 1908 when he first showed up in Texas from Alabama in a covered wagon. He ended up in Harlingen, a town in the far southern toe of the state, in a fertile zone of the Rio Grande Valley on the border with Mexico, a short distance from the Gulf. He started out building shacks for migrant workers and digging irrigation ditches.

Fast forward to 2011, when the company celebrated its seventy-fifth year in business. The December 7 issue of *Construction Today*, an engineering trade magazine, carried a glowing profile of the company and its storied history. Ballenger's annual revenue had grown to $105 million thanks to dozens of major road, water, aviation, and other infrastructure joint ventures, the majority in Texas. The writer began her article by noting, "Ballenger Construction heavy equipment is a common sight along the bridges, highways, and airport runways of South Texas."

Exactly one year later, Ballenger filed for bankruptcy. On a single day, it ordered all its employees to lay down their tools and vacate twenty-two major infrastructure construction sites in South Texas. Exactly what went wrong isn't clear but it appears the company got caught needing to refinance just as the credit markets dried up. In its initial bankruptcy filing, the company could only estimate its debt—as high as $50 million—and listed assets of $50,000.

This might have been a colossal financial mess had it not been for the fact that in every case Ballenger had been required by law to purchase default insurance, called a surety bond, against just such a risk. Two weeks after Ballenger's work force was laid off, days before Christmas, the Texas Department of Transportation announced that the surety companies who'd guaranteed Ballenger's performance had already arranged for work to restart the following month. The statement added, "It's important to note, there will be NO additional cost to taxpayers for work required as part of these contracts."

The same holds true for Modern Continental and Boston's Big Dig project. A case study of the company's contracts for the Big Dig was funded by the Transportation Research Board of the National Academies of Sciences, Engineering, and Medicine. It describes how surety bonding companies stepped in when the contractor got into trouble, providing oversight and financing required to finish the work. The authors concluded that the company was driven into bankruptcy not by the Big Dig but by poor performance in its other businesses. As for the highway project: "Ultimately, all of the contracts ... were completed, and, in the aggregate, returned profit to the company."

Government is not structured to be an engine of innovation, spending tax dollars on experiments. That's the job of the private sector.

Surety bonds posted by private partners are the reason that large-scale infrastructure projects can get done and they are required for most federal projects. The Miller Act of 1935 was passed by Congress in the midst of the Franklin Roosevelt administration's response to the Great Depression—a cornucopia of gargantuan infrastructure contracts for the building of highways, dams, electrical grids, and other stimulus programs. The Act currently covers contracts exceeding $100,000 and requires contractors to obtain performance bonds as well as payment bonds "for the protection of all persons supplying all labor and materials in the prosecution of the work."

Between 2000 and 2016, the surety industry paid out more than $12 billion in losses plus covering the expenses of financing troubled contractors, hiring experts to shepherd troubled projects to completion, and paying subcontractors and suppliers. Surety bonds are a little like auto insurance that guarantees to replace your totaled car with one of equal value. You can own a car without buying the added coverage, but a contractor hoping to bid on infrastructure joint ventures won't get far without it. In addition to the federal law, many states have adopted similar legislation.

Elected officials will support a new idea, but want to be sure constituents will also support it and them.

For most construction companies working in the US, surety bonding is essential to their survival. In order to satisfy stringent underwriting standards, a private contractor needs a strong balance sheet and a long record of performance. And the surety requirement is often the reason some projects don't get done.

"It's all about capacity, capital, and character," says Joanne S. Brooks, vice president and counsel of The Surety & Fidelity Association of America, a trade association that promotes the use of fidelity and surety bonds to protect public and private interests.

Because P3s were developed outside of the US, the performance security most foreign contractors are familiar with are letters of credit (LOCs) which, according to Brooks, "don't make strategic financial sense to American contractors who have built their companies using bonding capacity based on the strength of their balance sheets." LOCs tend to be on-balance-sheet transactions whereas with surety credit, contractors don't have to tie up their own capital. Surety underwriters look at the enterprise as a whole rather than focusing on specific projects.

The Too-Big-To-Fail Myth

Brooks says a common misconception she encounters is the too-big-to-fail notion. "That just simply isn't true. There are graveyards filled with large contractors who have gone out of business."

She notes that many of the largest infrastructure companies, especially from other countries, have banking divisions that provide financing. Few public executives involved in partnerships with these large global companies have the experience to be able to untangle such interrelated transactions.

"They may not understand in those situations that if something goes wrong, it's going to go wrong on both sides—the work and the financing. Sureties," says Brooks, "do the due diligence that no one else is capable of."

On the state level, surety requirements vary. Although the majority of states have enacted legislation that requires bonds or some kind of performance security, some states make it optional. For example, a contractor on the Interstate 69 tollway project in Indiana who defaulted had a payment bond covering only 5 percent of the risk, and a performance bond covering only 25 percent.

Brooks offers a warning about all the work that's expected to come down the pike in the next few years as the infrastructure revolution picks up steam.

"In an economy where we have a lot of work and we have so much infrastructure work that needs to be done, most contractors who go out of business will do so because they take on too much work. Some companies may be tempted to bite off more than they can chew. All public procurement officials should educate themselves on surety bonds and be able to discern which contractors meet the capital, capacity, and character criteria for coverage."

7 Infrastructure Goes To School

I nfrastructure joint ventures aren't just for large-scale projects like highways, sewer plants, and airports. Without attracting much press, there has been a lot of activity on the campuses of the nation's public universities, driven by demand and desperation. In the lean years following the Great Recession, almost all fifty state legislatures took an axe to higher education budgets.

All but four states are spending less per student now than they did before the recession, according to the nonpartisan Center on Budget and Policy Priorities. Average declines between 2008 and 2016 range from 15 percent to 30 percent, with states like Arizona and Illinois showing per-student spending down more than 50 percent.

The bread and butter of joint university ventures is student housing and it has quietly become a very big

Although plagued by problems, Boston's Big Dig highway project had been insured against failure.

business. Austin, Texas–based American Campus Communities Inc., a publicly traded real estate investment trust, is the largest private dormitory developer and manager in the country, owning and/or managing more than 200 properties with about 130,000 beds at the end of 2016. Compared to a ranking that year of US hotels by trade journal *Hotel News Now*, American Campus's room count was tied with the fourth-largest hospitality chain in the country, and three times the size of the fifth largest, Hyatt.

Typical Dormitory Projects

In the typical arrangement, a developer leases property from a public university and then finances the design and construction to the school's specifications. When the building stage is complete, the contractor has a long-term management contract, recovering its investment from dorm fees. The staff responsible for supervising students and managing dorm life work for the university, just as they do when schools build and operate facilities on their own. To students and staff, there's no difference.

Universities negotiate with their private partners to come up with fees that are as affordable and competitive as possible while also meeting the return expectations of investors. At a time when one in seven college applicants can't afford their first-choice school, enrollment growth is slowing, and operating costs are rising faster than revenue, CFOs at every public college have to work with sharp pencils.

As with highway and other major contracts, there are penalties for performance failures, and incentives for delivering early and/or under budget. Schools usually get a lump sum payment up front before the project begins as well as annual income from lease payments. At the end of the contract the operator is obligated to turn the property over to the university in good condition. Generations of college students will take their toll on dorms, so the private manager has an incentive to construct or upgrade existing facilities on a build-to-last basis.

Higher Ed Collateral Benefits

Beyond dorms, joint ventures often have the potential for collateral benefits, like facilitating the financing and construction of redevelopment projects, according to researchers Darryl G. Greer and Michael W. Klein. Writing in *Trusteeship Magazine* in 2016, they reported, "Mixed-use facilities connecting colleges to their towns benefit local businesses and residents as well as students, faculty, and college staff. For example, Kent State University is partnering with the city of Kent, Ohio, and private developers on a $110-million, 500,000-square-foot project that includes a building for its College of Architecture and Environmental Design; retail and office space; and a transit center."

Metropolitan State University in Denver entered into a joint venture with an operator of a chain of SpringHill Suites, a Marriott brand, to build a hotel on an empty spot on the school's campus. Part of the deal was a state-of-the-art "hospitality learning center" with a culinary demonstration theater for students pursuing degrees in food service and lodging.

In 2013, MSU President Stephen M. Jordan reported that average occupancy in the hotel was about 75 percent—above the industry average—with more than a dozen sellout nights. "Our room rate is $150 per night, $25 more than we originally thought we could get. Our goal is that 80 percent of the positions in the hotel will be filled by our students. After graduating from our Hospitality, Tourism and Events program with

Surety bonds posted by private partners are the reason large-scale projects can get done.

experience at SpringHill Suites, students will be ready to take management positions in other hotels."

The City University of New York's School of Social Work was facing a crisis when its landlord announced that the building they occupied was going to be put on the market. The school needed to find a new home. In a complex but creative transaction, the school entered into a joint venture with two philanthropic institutions and a private developer to build the $110 million Lois V. and Samuel J. Silberman School of Social Work. CUNY negotiated a barter deal in which the developer ended up owning the old building in exchange for putting up the new one. The Brodsky Organization finished the school's new home just fourteen months after groundbreaking, at about $20 million under budget.

Ohio State's Energy Management Venture

Ohio State, third-largest public university in the country by enrollment, recently launched an innovative energy management joint venture with a consortium including Dutch firm ENGIE Services and private equity firm Axium Infrastructure. ENGIE will manage and operate all the heating, cooling, and power systems on the Columbus, Ohio, main campus, a city of 45,000 students plus staff, in countless buildings on 1,775 acres—twice the size of New York's Central Park.

The operations and maintenance contract was set at fifty years and valued at $1.165 billion. That included a $1.015 billion advance payment to the university and a $150 million commitment "to support academics in specific areas requested by students, faculty, and staff during the bidding process."

In exchange, ENGIE will have long-term predictable cash flow from selling energy and from management fees to pay investors a competitive rate of return for the risk they took. The university expects academic collaborations with ENGIE that will "produce sustainable energy solutions from discoveries made here at Ohio State ... increase student financial aid ... endow new faculty positions and invest in sustainability and staff development."

In 2013, Ohio State also signed a first-of-its-kind deal with Queensland Investment Corporation (QIC) to lease 36,000 on-campus parking spaces for fifty years. The school got an advance payment of $438 million for its endowment fund. QIC manages and maintains the parking facilities and collects

For most construction companies working in the US, surety bonding is essential to their survival.

the fees. The choice, according to one official, was simple. "Our core strength as a university is not running parking facilities. We should focus on what we're really good at and hire others to do what they're really good at."

The Ohio State joint ventures illustrate how, in a closed system like a university—less affected by the ebb and flow of election cycles—it's possible to make long-range plans with more certainty and flexibility. Investors are attracted to investments backed by the extended, predictable, essentially guaranteed cash flow of a permanent and prized state institution.

Texas A&M Partners For A New Data Center

At Texas A&M, the nation's second-largest public university, Chancellor John Sharp has overseen some of the most ambitious and creative joint ventures in the country. He says most of A&M's dorms have been built as joint ventures. The most recent, built on vacant land that had been used for grazing about two dozen horses, was structured as a simple ground lease and is the largest student housing project in the nation, adding 3,400 beds in one fell swoop. The university received $18 million on signing and will receive lease payments of $10 million a year for the next thirty-two years.

"Everything that produces cash flow we first put through the public-private partnership review process to see if it fits," Sharp says.

The next big project is scheduled to be a data center that will be one of the largest in Texas and give A&M students hands-on experience studying topics like cyber security. Sharp says major data services and computer makers were eager to bid on it, especially after 2017's Hurricane Harvey exposed the need for secure backup systems during natural disasters. He forecasts the university will realize between $5 million and $10 million a year in revenue from a project that will cost the school nothing to build or maintain, will add to its curriculum, and will prepare students to graduate workforce-ready for real jobs in a growing industry.

Sharp says A&M's embrace of joint venture projects has also paid off by easing the school's cash flow and saving money on debt service. "Because we have made public-private collaborations a priority, we've shifted debt [and risk] off our balance sheet and earned a triple-A credit rating."

One of A&M's most recent joint venture projects is a 250-room hotel being built next to the Kyle Field stadium where the school's fabled football team plays. The university has an army of active alumni who are fiercely loyal fans, many of them successful in business. In addition to the expected benefits of a public-private partnership, the university leveraged the project by auctioning off guaranteed reservations on game weekends for the next decade in return for tax-deductible donations ranging from $100,000 to $475,000.

8 The Global Imperative

nother nontraditional category with outsized potential has been opening up in the building, upgrade, and maintenance of airports, essential to the economic vitality of any city and for many nations. Airports today actively compete with each other and now face new competition from formerly sleepy regional airports that are expanding and being upgraded to handle larger planes and volume.

As measured by the most recent annual survey by Skytrax World Airport Awards, the state of US airports is an embarrassment. Based on nearly 14 million questionnaires completed by passengers from 105 countries, the top-ranked American airport—26th out of 100—was Cincinnati.

Airport infrastructure contracts tend to go to large global companies that specialize in construction, maintenance, and operations. These companies have the advantage of decades of experience and expertise, and are able to bring funding and ensure efficient operation and modern facilities. Repayment to the private sector investor comes from revenue sharing and fees for ongoing management and operations.

Other joint ventures take a non-revenue-producing asset, usually property, and find a private sector partner to develop it. These types of engagements often involve upgraded urban facilities such as city parks, affordable-housing developments, new retail establishments on once idle public property, or new sports and performing arts venues. Repayment of the initial investment is generated from new revenue produced or from maintenance and operating fees.

Water treatment is another public utility that attracts major international firms with decades of experience in solving problems and inventing solutions, especially in less-developed parts of the world where epidemic diseases are a constant threat. These vendors offer a value proposition that manifests itself in projects being completed on time and on budget. Because the private sector partner is contracted to operate and maintain the plants it builds, there is an incentive to make them efficient and durable.

Under used and mothballed military bases across the country—about 125 in all—are being developed by the communities where they are located into joint venture housing, office parks, public parks, and other uses. Tax-exempt acreage is put on the rolls, generating tax revenue and all the other benefits of increased economic activity.

Certain citizen services that were traditionally handled by public employees in government offices are also being increasingly outsourced through collaborative partnerships with private sector firms that make large capital investments in new facilities, equipment, technology, and resources. Public agencies whose operational functions are run by a private partner usually include provisions that require private sector partners to offer jobs to public employees first, at comparable rates of pay. Private partners are often able to offer former public employees better benefits and greater career options.

How The US Fell So Far Behind

The US is late to the party when it comes to partnerships largely because the United States had invested heavily in infrastructure for decades, beginning in the Great Depression and through World War II. In the 1950s, President Dwight D. Eisenhower, who had been the general in charge of the defeat of Nazi Germany and was impressed with the military usefulness of its autobahns, proposed the national interstate highway system. It was a massive public works project that took thirty-five years to complete, ended up costing more than half a trillion dollars (adjusted for inflation), and played a major role in driving the prosperity the US has enjoyed in the years since.

In the 1960s, the cost of the Vietnam War and of President Lyndon Johnson's Great Society programs, combined with inflation, brought a halt to further funding for large infrastructure projects. Time slowly took its toll, and when major repairs and upgrades became necessary, most public officials assumed that federal infrastructure spending would pick up again. They reasoned that the federally funded highways would receive federally funded maintenance.

The federal government expected to be able to rely on fuel and related taxes to pay for it all but that revenue couldn't keep pace with costs. Today there is no support in Washington for making up the difference.

Hotel companies partner with hospitality degree programs and tech companies with tech programs to prepare work-ready graduates.

In sharp contrast, while America was building itself up, the rest of the world's infrastructure development was hobbled by autocratic and state-directed economies and interrupted by the disruption and devastation of war, both shooting and Cold.

Governments in Europe and elsewhere lacked the political will and the ability to fund major infrastructure projects on their own. For decades, private sector capital has been essential for public projects to be completed and maintained. While we were neglecting our infrastructure, the rest of the world was busy building and innovating.

Government officials across the US are now getting the message that the bank of Uncle Sam is no longer a reliable lender. State and local levels of government are turning to public-private ventures as the only way forward, especially in a period of intense anti-government, anti-tax sentiment among voters.

Those who are holding out for the federal government to step in and underwrite their critical infrastructure projects should be advised—that's not going to happen. In most cases, they'll have to learn the art of leveraging what funds they have and shedding risk they don't need through joint ventures.

At Stake: America's Competitive Edge

The stakes couldn't be higher for America's ability to compete on the world stage. The most dramatic example is what has happened in China in just the past decade or so. It all started with the 2008 Olympics in Beijing.

Anyone who has visited China recently is immediately impressed by the many massive, modern, awe-inspiring public works. The country boasts brand new, state-of-the-art airports; enormous rail stations; gleaming new high-speed rolling stock; new commuter rail networks; a sophisticated highway network; power grids using the latest, most efficient generating and distribution technologies, including the largest wind-power base in the world; a robust and

"We focus on what we're good at and hire others to do what they're good at."

ubiquitous wireless communications network; modern port facilities; and oil and gas pipelines that will one day make it possible to pump Persian Gulf products thousands of miles overland to China.

On a visit in June 2017, Goldman Sachs chief executive Lloyd Blankfein was so impressed by the sophistication of China's airports, roads, and cell service that he was inspired to tweet, "US needs to invest in infrastructure to keep up!"

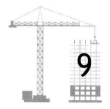 **9** Prophets Before Profits

I n spite of the urgency of our infrastructure crisis, and in spite of the success of most joint ventures in other countries, too many public officials in the US remain hesitant or wary. Skeptics cite projects that were flawed, like Chicago's parking meters, or perceived failures like Indiana's seventy-five-year tolled roadway project.

Some public officials may see the benefits of a joint venture but are intimidated by their inexperience, or they are unwilling to risk stirring up controversy. On one hand, they must navigate the unfamiliar rough-and-tumble world of commerce and, on the other, face anti-government activists decrying what they consider to be giveaways that circumvent democracy.

Jennifer L. Hara, North American manager of public-private partnerships for the Institute for Public-Private Partnerships (IP3), says, "The concept that causes public officials the most discomfort is the misimpression that a public-private partnership means turning a public service into a private enterprise."

Partnership—Not The Same As Privatization

Well-planned and executed public-private partnerships are structured to protect taxpayers. Ownership of public assets always remains with government. Citizens and taxpayers remain in charge by way of their government representatives, regulatory and enforcement agencies, oversight authority, and in the fine print in contracts that hold contractors responsible for a long list of factors. Nevertheless, large-scale infrastructure undertakings—with their huge budgets, long timelines, and political crosswinds—attract attention and generate controversy.

The Institute for P3s provides partners with consulting, knowledge-base, and workforce development services. It is operated by Tetra Tech, a leading global infrastructure consulting and engineering firm, to help contractors and their public clients become astute at developing, evaluating, negotiating, and executing successful joint ventures. People come from all over the world to take seminars and attend conferences at the Institute's headquarters in suburban Washington, DC.

"Everyone we work with understands that the private sector must generate some degree of profit," says IP3's Hara. "That can be challenging for those whose careers are rooted in the conviction that only government should deliver public services, and that it can do so more frugally."

P3s can help ease cash flow issues and lower the burden of debt service.

Cheaper, however, isn't always less expensive in the long run. You can't compare a publicly financed and managed project with a joint venture without considering the hidden value to government in transferring risk. In a true public-private joint venture, the private partner assumes virtually all the risk of failure. Less risk means healthier public balance sheets, better credit ratings, cheaper debt service, and fewer "black swans" that could lead to cuts in other services and/or higher taxes. With less risk, infrastructure planners and engineers can lay out long-term goals with greater certainty that the projects they plan will actually get done.

The New Gold Standard: Value For Money

The emerging gold standard for evaluating proposed joint ventures on a dollar-for-dollar basis is called "value for money" (VFM). A value for money calculation is done to help public entities determine whether a public-private partnership is the most efficient way to finance a project. The analysis, a public and transparent process, takes into account all direct and indirect costs—designing, building, financing, operating, maintaining, and risk assumption. Then a comparison is done based on delivery method, as a joint venture versus a traditional model. In most cases, the result of this analysis makes the choice clear and helps gain support from taxpayers and other stakeholders.

It's often tempting for public agencies that are self-funding and have lean budgets to opt for less robust interim fixes for a worn-out bridges for example, putting off upkeep. But a patched up or cheaper bridge will wear out faster and require more major repairs in the future, an inefficient and more costly tactic.

When government partners with private capital, the private partner is motivated to build a bridge that is durable enough to handle future demand; get it done in the shortest period of time; design it to withstand the ravages of time and require minimal maintenance costs; satisfy the public's expectations for efficiency and safety; and meet its contractual obligation to turn it over to the taxpayers thirty or so years later in good condition.

Partnerships Help Reduce Surprises

As a result, in the most successful joint ventures there should be no unpleasant financial surprises for the public partner. Contracts specify exactly what the cost is going to be and any problems that pop up are the responsibility and expense of the contractor. If the project is a new government office building, the company that gets the design-build-maintain contract is likely to make sure the HVAC system is the most efficient and reliable.

In the older, more traditional financing model, government is a customer, paying contractors to execute stages of a project, subject to change orders, cost overruns, labor problems, etc. When something goes wrong, government is on the hook. There is no way to transfer risk.

In the more modern, true joint ventures, the private partner puts up the capital to build infrastructure over which government ultimately retains control as well as delivering public services.

In cases where an asset does not generate revenue, the public partner lease-purchases it in installments over the life of the contract instead of having to load up the public balance sheet with debt. Joint ventures allow infrastructure projects to get started and be completed sooner. Without a joint venture, many of today's projects could never be launched.

Short of taking a crash MBA course on how the private sector operates, public sector officials should seek assistance from prophets—experienced, independent advisors who can evaluate the financial and logistical aspects of a project and help negotiate contracts that will stand the

US investing in infrastructure dropped off after the interstate highway system was completed in the 1960s.

test of time and stress. Public officials should also seek guidance on solicitation documents from procurement technicians when launching their first public-private partnership.

My mantra for public officials who are new to such partnerships is simple: A public-private partnership will be unlike anything you've ever done before. You should select an experienced financial advisor, a legal advisor, and a technical procurement advisor. The cost will be recouped many times over by the time the project is completed, the lease expires, and the asset is turned over to the public.

Mind The Knowledge Gap

Without experts by their sides, public partners risk knowledge gaps that private partners could exploit. A knowledge gap or oversight has so far cost Chicago about $75 million in refunds to its parking meter operator because of the overlooked provision requiring the city to pay a daily fine for meters taken out of service by civic events, roadwork, etc. Contract flaws like that are less likely to happen today as both public and private sectors are becoming more sophisticated about the process.

During my career I have had a chance to know, work with, and observe many public executives. I was one myself for many years. I know it can be daunting for an agency head who is worried about loss of control of essential public services to sit face to face with an experienced sales representative from a Fortune 100 company that has been involved in dozens of public-private partnerships. Questions that should be asked and concerns that should be raised can easily

China has been busy building a robust infrastructure network that challenges the US to keep up.

be brushed aside. There is no end to the headaches that can result. Experienced advisors are worth their cost many times over. Only the most experienced public official should attempt to launch a large P3 engagement without such assistance..

Public sector partners should enter into discussions about joint ventures armed with knowledge and with confidence because they are in charge and in control. "These are your assets," I remind them. "This is your project. Don't let yourself be rushed or pushed around."

A P3 Is Like A Marriage

In spite of how ill-fitting a private sector partner initially appears to public officials, "They get it quite quickly," says IP3's Hara. "Public officials and executives tend to be senior careerists with families, so they can relate when I compare these partnerships to a marriage. There are good days, bad days, disagreements, compromises. But in the end it's a long-term commitment to a relationship and everybody has to focus on making it work."

A key element to success is flexibility. Hara advises, "Do your best to negotiate all of the what-ifs you can possibly imagine, but remember that your contract is a living document. If things change, be flexible and open."

Another key element Hara cites is knowing how to present a proposed partnership agreement to public constituents in a way that highlights why it's an appropriate, economically sound solution to an infrastructure problem. This is especially so when the problem is urgent and it's the only workable solution.

The Transportation Infrastructure Crisis

An urgent problem that the majority of Americans confront every day is transportation, in all its forms. While nations in Western Europe and elsewhere have been experiencing slowing or zero population growth, population growth in America has been steady. As of 2017, the US population was estimated at about 325 million, an increase since 2000 of about 40 million.

The bulk of the growth has been, and is expected to continue to be, in the largest metropolitan areas where the problems of worn-out highways, mass transit, and water resource issues reach back many decades. As measured by INRIX, a big-data research firm, three of the four longest car commutes in the world—among a thousand cities—were American. US cities made up half the top twenty where motorists spent a greatest amount of time sitting in traffic jams.

Public officials considering transportation partnerships should seek out experts and consultants who can guide them through the process, keeping the playing field level with investment groups that, before they commit, conduct extensive due diligence. All investors look closely at revenue models demand projections, the health of the public entity, the transparency of the procurement process, and the capabilities of the political leader on any project. That's where the greatest transfer of risk occurs.

P3s can offer hidden value to government in the form of reduced risk.

Part of the vetting process is the detailed investigation that surety underwriters do before agreeing to guarantee a project against failure. Advisors who help public officials plan and develop an attractive and fair solicitation process can enhance the quality of bidders that the public entity is able to attract.

Highway 130: A Case Study

The value of all this oversight by both partners becomes apparent when something goes awry, as it did a few years ago in Texas with the build-out of a crucial section of a new tollway between Austin and San Antonio. The new tollway was built to relieve congestion on an older interstate route that had become clogged with cargo-laden trucks, a result of the post-NAFTA boom in US-Mexico trade.

The Highway 130 project added an alternative, limited-access parallel route with speed limits up to 85 miles an hour. At the northern end of this route, the state capitol of Austin was becoming the business hotspot it is today, attracting technology giants like Dell, Apple, and IBM. The growth in population and business activity was explosive.

Cintra, a large international developer of transportation infrastructure, partnered in 2006 with Texas-based Zachry Construction to win a $1.3 billion contract to complete two key toll segments of Highway 130. The partnership entity signed with the state what was then the longest such contract in Texas history—fifty years. The SH 130 Concession Company (Cintra, Zachry, and others) agreed to finance, design, build, operate, and maintain the road for half a century in return for a share of the toll revenue. The coalition based its projected revenues on a demand study that proved to be flawed.

Almost as soon as the award was announced, there were complaints about having to pay a toll for the public road. Traffic demand was less than anticipated. A year after the deal was made, the credit markets began to seize up. A year later, the economy went into the steepest tailspin since the Great Depression. Traffic declined even more as truckers looking to cut costs switched to existing toll-free roads. Congestion increased and toll revenue slumped 30 percent below projections.

Caught between anemic cash flow, flawed demand projections, and tight credit markets, the consortium ended up filing for reorganization under Chapter 11 of the bankruptcy law. Opponents of the project claimed that taxpayers would end up holding the bag for the company's mistakes. They were wrong.

The deal negotiated by the Texas Department of Transportation shifted all of the financial and performance responsibility onto the private consortium, which was fully bonded. "We knew that [Highway] 130 was tough," a former state highways official later recalled, but then, "Somebody else said, 'We'll take that risk.'"

In spite of its financial woes, the SH 130 Concession Company kept the highway open while it restructured its debt. Brian Cassidy, an attorney who worked on the bankruptcy and reorganization, later told a reporter, "One of the criticisms that you hear periodically about public-private partnerships is that they somehow put the public at risk of having to cover private sector obligations. The fact is, if the agreements are structured correctly—and this is an example of one that was—then that risk to the public sector doesn't really exist."

Rough Roads Can Still Lead To Success

Although the private consortium couldn't make a go of the Highway 130 project and ended up selling its interest to another investor group, Texas motorists ended up with a beautiful new toll road, a thirty-year maintenance agreement, and an income source from its share of the toll revenue.

Such outcomes are not uncommon. San Antonio is another metropolitan area that has grown rapidly in the past decade or so. The city's most pressing issue was securing a stable water supply to withstand droughts and accommodate continuing growth. In spite of big strides in getting people to cut back waste and to conserve, demand was in danger of outstripping the ability of the Edwards Aquifer, which is the primary source of the area's water..

In 2015, city leaders in San Antonio approved a contract worth

Public sector officials need prophets— independent advisors to evaluate projects and contracts.

about $3 billion to buy up to 16.3 billion gallons of water a year for thirty years from another aquifer in north central Texas. The agreement included construction of a dedicated 142-mile pipeline, to be built as part of a joint venture with the San Antonio Water System (SAWS) and a consortium including Texas-based BlueWater Systems, Garney Construction, and Abengoa Water USA, an affiliate of a multinational infrastructure company based in Seville, Spain.

SAWS negotiated a contract that stipulated no payments would be made to the private sector consortium until the project began delivering water. The agreement protected the city from any financial obligations incurred by the water system. The contract states unequivocally that SAWS "shall have no obligation to provide financing for the project or for any project company-requested capital modifications." At the end of the thirty-year agreement, the public will own the pipeline.

Before construction even got started, the prime contractor parent ran into financial troubles and ended up filing for Chapter 11 bankruptcy. In the process, it sold most of its majority stake to one of the other consortium partners, but the transaction did not interfere with the progress of the project or impact taxpayers in any way.

The San Antonio Water System joint venture is instructive for a number of reasons. The system (SAWS) has the right to overrule any change in ownership of the consortium. It retains the power to inspect the work, impose sanctions, and enforce compliance if it deems maintenance of the pipeline or quality control is below standards.

The Availability Revenue Model

SAWS payments to the consortium are based on the availability of water. Availability is a revenue model that is becoming common in many public-private partnership contracts. A city that enters into a venture for construction and maintenance of a performing arts center can make its payments to the consortium contingent on the facility's availability and the quality of maintenance, which is specified in the agreement ahead of time. Should the public partner determine that the quality has slipped or the facility is unavailable when needed or fails to meet maintenance quality standards, payment to the private partner can be suspended.

To skirt the problem of imprecise demand projections—a factor in revenue-based projects like parking garages, toll roads, and entertainment venues—payments based on availability are used in joint venture contracts to lessen the risk to private sector investors. Regardless of demand, as long as the asset is available, maintained, and safe, the contractor receives a guaranteed minimum availability payment.

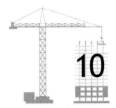

10 Partnership Basics

N ot all infrastructure projects lend themselves to joint ventures. The first step for public officials is to put a potential project through a simulation to see if it meets the goals and manifests the advantages of a partnership. Broadly, those goals would be:

- Leverage private investment and public tax dollars to make possible major projects that might otherwise not be possible using public funds and debt alone;

- Speed up delivery of major improvements;

- Shift as much risk as possible from taxpayers to investors;

- Guarantee or incentivize on-time, on-budget completions;

- Gain access to private sector expertise, capabilities, knowledge, and innovations;

- Conserve public debt capacity and enhance credit ratings by

A Texas tollway project highlights the risk of relying on demand and revenue forecasts.

moving financial burdens off the public balance sheet;

- Shift the burden of long-term operation and maintenance responsibilities to experienced private partners;
- Create jobs and stimulate greater economic activity.

Essential Questions When Considering a P3

The questions listed are easy ones. The harder ones include the following:

- Why consider a public-private partnership in the first place? The answer is usually a funding issue and access to private sector expertise that government needs.
- Is there statutory authority? Some entities already have it and some need to get it.
- Is the project big enough to justify a joint venture engagement? Infrastructure partnerships typically are $100 million or more. Larger projects attract more interest from private capital and large, experienced contractors. If projected costs are below that, a possible tactic to attract interest is to consolidate several smaller projects into one partnership. This often produces unexpected benefits when the sum turns out to be greater than its parts. A new courthouse plus a parking garage, some retail space, and access road upgrades is more likely to attract a suitable bid and end up being a big boost to a town's economy.
- Who will serve as the political champion? It is essential that the effort is led with conviction and determination. The leader may be an elected official, but projects can also be led by an internal champion—an agency executive with clout, for example—who has a public presence and the full support of the board, commission, or other governing body.
- Could the project be successful without private sector capital? This is an important question to answer early on because it will be asked by others, repeatedly, by supporters and opponents.

- Are there assets or other funds available that could augment private sector capital investment? Some public entities contribute land and/or grant funds to a project. The example given in an earlier chapter is a good one: Washington, DC, got a new, much-needed elementary school for free in exchange for granting the builder a lease on an adjacent vacant lot to put up a new apartment building.

- What is the revenue model that will repay the private partner's capital investment plus a competitive rate of return? Not all infrastructure projects generate revenue. A serious and detailed value for money analysis should be part of the process of determining how government is going to finance a project.

- Is there a risk-reduction benefit and, if so, what is the value? Part of the "what if" analysis is pinning down what risks the public entity will retain and which will be transferred to the private partner.

- Will outside advisors be required? If so, in which disciplines and how will they be procured? Public entities embarking on their first partnership *must* retain seasoned experts with experience in the areas the project touches on. Most public officials, even those with experience, hire external advisors..

San Antonio's water project highlights many best-practice elements.

- What areas of expertise and/or experience are available within the public entity? Every agency has some internal expertise that can be tapped and it should be identified early in the planning stages. It is also a good idea to evaluate whether or not the internal people with expertise will have other responsibilities that should be reassigned if they are tapped to work on the project.

- Have all the risks been identified? A list of risks should be assembled at the start and evaluated again with external advisors. Risk transfer is a core component of any public-private engagement, so quantifying it in detail is an important part of the process.

- Has a civic outreach plan been developed? If so, will it be overseen internally or externally? This is an often overlooked component but is high on the list of best practices. All communication should be handled by experienced professionals with emphasis on transparency and on messaging that highlights the practicality or necessity of a collaborative engagement. Communication efforts should include all stakeholders and interested parties, not just citizens, taxpayers, and the media. An effective community outreach effort should continue throughout the life of the project.

- What is the anticipated timeline from start to finish? Every project is different but internal expectations should be compared with objective projections when the planning process is complete, before timelines are committed to contractually.

- How will transparency be built into the process? Public entities and taxpayers have a right to know the details of partnerships. Transparency is important throughout the process, but especially when a project is launched. How will issues about transparency be handled among the partners throughout the duration of the engagement?

- Finally, how will success be defined? Public officials should define the elements they will consider when answering.

Virginia Shares Two Decades of P3 Experience

To illustrate why this process is so important, consider two road projects in Virginia's Hampton Roads region, an area of rivers and peninsulas that stretches about ninety miles from the coastal city of Norfolk to the inland state capital, Richmond. Hampton Roads describes the harbor that is bordered by the cities of Norfolk and Hampton and is home to the US Fleet Forces Command, the largest naval station in the world.

Virginia has had more than two decades of experience with public-private partnerships, ever since the legislature first authorized them as an infrastructure mechanism in the 1990s. The first project example is a proposed new fifty-five-mile toll road linking Norfolk with Interstate 95, the main north-south artery that runs from Miami to Maine's border with Canada. The existing link, Interstate 64, is considered to be in a failing state of repair, and it was a question of whether to rebuild and widen it or repair it and build a new tollway.

The new tollway plan was originally proposed as a public-private partnership but "morphed into a more conventional contract," according to a report by journalist Daniel C. Vock. "The state hired a private contractor to design and build the new road but, crucially, [the state] assumed the risk in case necessary [federal environmental] permits did not come through."

Unfortunately, those permits did not come through and the project had to be halted before construction had begun. The contract was cancelled, and the state was out of pocket $290 million with nothing to show for it. Without second-guessing the decisions that went into such a risky-sounding venture, it is a valuable cautionary tale that all public officials ought to think about before considering taking on any risk that can be avoided.

The other Virginia project that ran into controversy was the proposed public-private partnership to improve the 3.5 mile Hampton Roads Bridge-Tunnel, part of an interstate highway that carries traffic under the main shipping channels for the Hampton Roads harbor and naval base.

The bridge-tunnel was first opened in 1957, designed for a maximum flow of 77,000 vehicles a day, and has been free ever since the ribbon-cutting. Today the crossing handles as many as 100,000 vehicles a day, and it suffered a flood in 2009 and a damaging and dangerous vehicle fire in 2016.

A consortium won a long-term public-private partnership

contract with the state to finance, deliver, operate, and maintain the metro area's two tunnels and a bridge; to build on two more lanes to the longest and most important tunnel; and to extend an arterial expressway. The plan was based on a financial model that included the unpopular introduction of tolls. Like the flawed Chicago parking PPP, the contract also included a provision that could have the unintended result of making future improvements in the area's highway network difficult to plan and more costly.

Headlines generated by the two projects caused Virginia officials to tap the brakes a bit on PPPs. A 2015 Department of Transportation report on public-private partnerships stirred debate by speculating whether Virginia, with its AAA bond rating, could do better on its own because it can borrow more cheaply than the private sector. But a nonprofit regional transportation planning group was quick to debunk the notion, pointing out the absence in the report of a value-for-money analysis and noting that tying up public capital, instead of letting investors assume the risk, limits the availability of public funds for other projects.

With some adjustments to the regulations governing P3s, Virginia continues to build on its experience, which has been positive. Testifying before Congress in 2017, Virginia's Transportation Secretary Aubrey Layne said, "I think we've started to do P3s right, and Virginia is a leader in those deals. I'm happy to share our experience with the nation."

11 Public Partner Checklist

The following are the basics for evaluating whether to pursue an infrastructure joint venture.

Preparation

- Verify that the repayment model on which the project financing is predicated is solid and likely to endure for the entire engagement, which can range from ten to seventy-five years.

- Identify which risks will be transferred to the private sector partner, and what risks the public agency is willing to retain. Most public officials transfer as much of their risk as they can, but in most joint ventures today, availability risk is shared in return for a share of the revenue.

- Explore and identify the ways in which the partnership will leverage private sector expertise. Anticipate questions from stakeholders, taxpayers, and the media about what private sector expertise is needed and why. Discussing this early in the process will help develop the messaging that will be important in generating support and buy-in later from all stakeholders..

- Objectively compare all other funding options to ensure that a private sector partnership is the best choice. Questions will be raised about why private sector capital is required and the answers must be accurate, plausible, convincing, and clear. All stakeholders should be able to understand why a partnership engagement is the most efficient method for procuring or improving the public asset.

- The gold standard evaluation model is the value for money (VFM) analysis described in Chapter 9. This analysis requires a public entity to list all associated costs of the project including designing, building, financing, operating, maintaining, and assuming project risks. Once all costs have been established, it's possible to make an apples to apples comparison among the competing delivery models to decide which is the most efficient and effective.

- Identify issues that will be important to each class of stakeholder, including citizens and internal staff. Public employees will typically be uncomfortable or distrustful about change. Constituents will want to know about implications for fees and taxes. Although labor union pension funds often invest in public-private partnerships, it will be very important to plan for issues related to union members' employment and benefits.

- List in detail all complications and obstacles that may and probably will need to be addressed—environmental, regulatory, political, etc.—and develop a strategy for overcoming them.

- Develop a detailed civic outreach plan and identify early which agency or individual(s)—internally or externally— will be responsible for overseeing it. The civic outreach plan should be treated as an evolving document but start with drafting answers to questions that will inevitably be asked.

- Create a timeline for the project. How long will it take to get regulatory authority, if that is required? What issues will be of concern to federal and other governmental entities? Questions are always raised about timelines and answers should be thoughtfully prepared and readily available. Projects that will take years to complete may discourage bids from highly competent private-partner prospects. If the public entity is transparent about the timeline and assertive about beginning the process, experienced private sector firms may be persuaded to give a project a second look.

- Identify and budget for outside advisors that may be needed. Most advisors will provide some preliminary advice and consultation early in the process. Meet with them and ask all the questions necessary to come away with a clear understanding of the services they provide, the projects they have handled, and how they charge for services. A solicitation document for external advisory services can be drafted at a later time.

After completing these preliminary tasks, whether to move forward with a PPP engagement should be a clear and easy choice and one that is reached with confidence. If the decision is to proceed, the first step should be to retain any outside advisors with financial, legal, and procurement expertise and experience.

An overlooked benefit of P3s is preserving public capital for other projects less suited for a partnership.

Almost all public entities retain external advisors, consultants who help develop feasibility studies; plan procurement criteria and processes; manage regulatory and environmental issues; and provide ongoing legal, financial, and technical guidance.

Public officials should interview multiple candidates in each discipline. The process is usually initiated with a Request for Qualifications (RFQ) or a Request for Interest (RFI). Here are some guidelines to consider when thinking about external consultants and advisors:

- What kind of qualifications and experience should advisors have?
- How will their fees be structured?
- How long will their services be needed?
- What types of assistance and expertise will be required?
- Who will oversee and/or manage the advisors?
- What will be the timeline for deliverables?
- Will travel will be required?

As mentioned earlier, public officials should bring in outside advisors for early discussions before any formal announcements are made about whether or not a project will be developed through a public-private engagement. Expect any decision to generate questions from the public. Have a plan in place and well-developed messaging ready to go. Anticipate issues and avoid causing confusion. Don't overreact to dissension. and err on the side of providing too much information so that you don't invite negative media attention.

Make a point of reading case studies to learn about potential pitfalls to avoid. Check with other public officials who have gone through the process. Most are willing to talk about their experience and they often welcome the opportunity to provide advice and good counsel to a peer.

All of this advance work—research, planning, evaluating, investigating, testing—are the foundations of a successful infrastructure joint venture.

Potential private partners are impressed when they meet public officials who have done their homework. It gives them confidence that a project has a good chance of success. Competition gives public officials more leverage in negotiations.

Infrastructure joint ventures, public-private partnerships, and all the permutations that are possible in such collaborations are the future. In the context of our infrastructure crisis, we cannot afford to fail.

The following chapters are aimed at helping all parties (public officials, private sector investors, and contractors) to understand the process even better. Potential partners on both sides will need to become more inovative in dealing with each other's culture, between the deliberative process of government and the competitive nature of commerce.

12 Start Small, Think Large

Large, experienced global contractors are generally interested in infrastructure projects with price tags starting at about $75 million. But it's possible to generate interest for smaller projects by being creative.

Bundling a number of smaller projects into a single solicitation is one way public officials have been successful at generating interest and competition for smaller projects. One of the most highly visible and talked about infrastructure bundles was put together in Pennsylvania, home of thousands of old, structurally deficient bridges.

Many of the bridges were located in suburban areas near cities that were once farmland. The outdated bridges were built as one- or two-lane single-span crossings of small creeks with an average length of fifty feet. They were designed for light traffic and the occasional herd of dairy cows. Other bridges were located in rural areas that are now hotspots for natural gas production and are used by heavy equipment needed to drill and maintain wells.

The volume of traffic and the weight of modern vehicles

and equipment have worn out many of these small bridges and the state Department of Transportation (PennDOT) has had to close some without having the money to fix or replace them. Unlucky residents separated from shopping centers, schools, and work places endured years of inconvenience and extended response times for fire, ambulance, and police services. The complaints piled up at PennDOT and in the inboxes of elected officials.

Pennsylvania Rapid Bridge Replacement Project

In 2012, the state legislature passed a law establishing a public-private transportation board within PennDOT to find joint venture solutions for bridges and other projects. One of the board's first proposals was the $1.1 billion Rapid Bridge Replacement Project, which bundled the rebuilding of more than 550 bridges into one infrastructure contract for design, construction, and twenty-eight years of maintenance. The winning bidder had to demonstrate that it could complete the construction phase in three years.

PennDOT estimated that the average cost for the state to replace just one of the small bridges was about $2 million and that if the department had repaired all of them under the standard process, it would take more than fifteen years. A public-private partnership contract, awarded in 2015 to a consortium, cut the average cost of rebuilding the bridges by nearly $500,000 each, a total savings of about $275 million. The work is ongoing but the state is projected to save many millions more in maintenance costs. The project was financed in part by an issue of tax-exempt bonds and the state will pay for it all by making scheduled availability payments. At the end of the twenty-eight years, the bridges will return to the PennDOT fold for maintenance and repair.

By the end of the 2017 construction season, the consortium, Plenary Walsh Keystone Partners, had begun work on about 60 percent of the bridges, with about half of the spans in the project completed and delivered. In the Digest section at the back of this book, you will find excerpts from documents related to the Rapid Bridge Replacement Project, including the initial credit assessment of the proposed bonds by Standard & Poors. The report gives a good look inside a joint venture from the perspective of risk assignment and exposure on both the public and private sides.

County and City Projects

Smaller projects are often found at the county and city levels of government. Cities and counties often consolidate projects to attract a wider field of bidders and to stimulate competition. The projects don't even have to be similar. Refurbishing downtown areas through P3 engagements that include multiple initiatives are common. Projects may include vertical construction, real estate development, transit, road expansion, broadband, and greenbelts.

Counties are using bundled joint venture engagements to build courthouses and administrative buildings that allow government agencies that have had to rent office space in other locations to be consolidated under one roof. These projects often include retail development, either within the facilities or on underused public property. Some counties use bundled joint ventures for road maintenance and snow removal.

As discussed in Chapter 7, universities and community colleges are using P3 engagements for the construction of student housing, new athletic facilities, parking garages, etc.

Austin (Texas) Community College partnered with real estate developers to expand its classroom capacity. The project was bundled with the purchase and renovation of an aging indoor mall. Office space was also developed and leased to high-tech firms interested in attracting student interns.

The partnership purchased adjacent property and

developed affordable condominiums for off-campus housing along with retail space. The project, in a section of the city that had been struggling economically, turned the neighborhood in one of the city's more desirable areas to live.

Availability Payments In Smaller Communities

In the past, the principal challenge for smaller communities that wanted to put together public-private partnerships was usually the problem of structuring a revenue repayment model. Today, availability payments are commonly used, especially for schools, prisons, rural hospitals, governmental agencies, and law enforcement. This model is wrapped around a lease and a long-term maintenance contract that includes the stipulation that if the facility or public asset is not available in prime condition—as specified in the contract—the public entity does not have to pay the full amount. The repayment model is basically structured like a lease, provided the facility is in prime condition and available as stipulated in the contract. Investors find these types of projects attractive as stable, long-term, low-risk investments.

In addition to small-city public-private partnerships for redevelopment, infrastructure, and amenity projects (stadiums, parks, entertainment venues), there are many partnerships involved in bringing broadband to rural underserved areas, upgrading water and wastewater facility operations, building green storm-water infrastructure, installing smart lighting or solar energy, and even providing public services such as roadside assistance for vehicles.

Advance work is the foundation of a successful infrastructure joint venture.

The city of Missoula, Montana (population 72,000) engaged a private sector partner to redevelop a riverfront property. A number of initiatives were consolidated, including construction of a conference center, retail development, a public plaza, and entertainment venues. The city used an asset-recycling revenue model, selling some of its riverfront property to developers.

Another small-city partnership in Salina, Kansas, a city of fewer than 50,000 residents, put together a $154 million downtown-redevelopment initiative that consolidated multiple revenue sources. The financing bundled $105 million in private funding with $19.1 million in state-issued bonds, $9.2 million in sales tax revenues, and $4.9 million in property tax revenue. The project delivered a downtown hotel, a field house, new streetscapes, theater improvements, a museum, and affordable housing units.

Burlington, Vermont (population 42,000), entered into a joint venture for a marina project on Lake Champlain. The private sector partner built a 160-boat-slip facility on public land and was given a contract to operate the marina for forty years. The city will receive lease payments plus revenue from public amenities on the property. The build-out included a parking lot and a public park. The project generates revenue for the city and the local economy got a huge economic boost that will last for decades.

Pubic Water Utilities

Cities with long-standing public water utilities have been turning to private sector partners when faced with having to replace aging equipment or build new water treatment plants to meet more stringent water quality standards. Common methods of repayment include dedicating a portion of revenue from user fees and installment payments for operations and maintenance over an extended period.

Water partnership proposals often stir up anxiety among residents who fear rate-gouging by a private operator. However, contracts are written so that water rates remain the province of the municipality, state public utility commission, or other authority. Water rates do not increase without public input and approval.

Public School P3s

School facilities, particularly K–12 education classrooms, are being built throughout the world with public-private partnerships. Classrooms are financed, designed, constructed, and then maintained by private sector contractors. The initial capital investment is repaid via a long-term availability contract as explained earlier. In order to continue receiving availability payments, the private partner must maintain the facilities to predetermined standards and make them available to school officials at all times.

The beauty of these types of partnerships is that school districts can get new, upgraded facilities with safety features, new technology, and expansion options at no initial cost. The repayment models stretch out for decades and are covered by lease payments.

With physical plants, facilities operations, and maintenance taken care of, school administrators and educators are able to focus all their attention on the students and their needs.

Many P3 engagements today call for this type of model to deliver learning centers with cutting-edge technology, indoor gymnasiums, swimming pools, kitchens, multipurpose centers, and after-school care and community rooms.

Bundling repair of more than 550 bridges expects to save about $275 million.

Ocean County, New Jersey, engaged in a partnership to obtain a new performing arts academy at its vocational technical school. A number of universities have used P3s to obtain research centers, student housing, and even to provide an online curriculum so that students can take classes from anywhere in the world.

Joint ventures will make it possible for cities of the future to become "smart"—by adding high-speed public Wi-Fi networks, LED street lights, and traffic signals linked with Internet of Things (IoT) technology. That will allow the collection of massive amounts of data that can be analyzed in real time and used for better planning in the future.

The possibilities and opportunities are endless. Partnerships and collaborative joint ventures will continue to expand and proliferate, helped along by advances in technology, support from the public, and capital from private investors seeking predictable income investments.

13 Civic Outreach

Once a decision has been made to seek a private sector partner for a public project, one of the first steps should be to start a dialogue with the public. That necessitates the development of a civic outreach plan.

The goal is to ensure transparency, generate public support, and build confidence in the leaders who will champion the effort. The first decision should be to evaluate whether to manage the outreach within or outsource it. If it is to be handled internally, a community planning group should be formed and put to work developing the project's message—defining the need and the rationale for entering into a public-private partnership to deliver the project. This planning team will be required to handle communications from the time the procurement documents are being developed until the project is completed.

P3s are being used to finance services such as smart lighting, solar energy, and even roadside assistance.

If a public entity lacks in-house expertise, a public relations/communications firm should be engaged, especially for large projects. Transparency and good communications for joint venture projects are important. Public entities should develop a budget that includes the outreach expense as a shared cost or, in some cases, shifts it completely to the winning bidder. Establishing community involvement early makes it less likely that a misunderstanding or contentious issues will result in controversy later..

The public sector working group should develop as much of the civic outreach plan as possible. Community leaders will be able to identify risks, obstacles, and questions that should be anticipated. They will also be more experienced in dealing with internal stakeholders, local media, citizen groups, and political factions. Whoever is directing the civic outreach plan must be in a position to marshal resources quickly to address issues as they emerge.

Internal employees are well equipped to help with early planning. They know the stakeholders, community influencers, organizations, user groups, and businesses leaders who should be engaged in the process. However, outside PR firms can better leverage media relationships, develop messages and materials, and organize and execute community events as requested or required.

Here are questions that the public team should consider carefully:

- What in-house resources, experience, and expertise are available to mount a vigorous, transparent, and effective effort? Most public bodies have a chief information officer and staff that handles public announcements, but how experienced is the staff in dealing with the media and handling events and developing messages that will be required? Who will represent the public partner in its interactions with the media? Is the designated political champion equipped and ready to handle inquiries, interviews, and editorial requests, or will those tasks be better handled by professionals? In the case of projects that depend on good communications with regulators and compliance officials, who will take the lead and how will those interactions be handled? Often this is done with internal staff working with experienced communication professionals.

Water utility P3 contracts are written so that rate setting authority remains with the public entity.

- If state or federal funds are to be used, or if there are environmental or permitting regulatory agencies involved, there may be a need for specific types of communications expertise. Would these efforts be more successful if outsourced to a contractor with experience in this area?

- Often the political champion for a P3 project is an elected official who is capable of dealing with the media. However, there should be a clear understanding about what media responsibilities the political champion is willing to assume. Most elected officials are too busy to write their own presentations and guest editorials. Some lack the internal resources to manage constituent and media questions. If that is the case, an outside firm is likely better equipped to manage the process and assist the political champion as requested.

- Does the public entity have marketing resources? It is unlikely there will be a need for sophisticated materials, but there will be a need for one-pagers that provide basic information and there will be a need for clear and targeted messaging. Who will develop the messages, format the one-pagers, and be responsible for ensuring that they are distributed effectively?

- How will transparency be handled and who will be responsible? Plans should be made to issue periodic progress reports once the project is launched. Websites and social media platforms are almost always employed. Information must be vetted for accuracy and be distributed in a timely manner. Questions should be encouraged and addressed promptly.

- Does the public entity have funding for the people and resources that will be required to implement a civic outreach plan? These costs are often built into the solicitation document. Most public officials wrap at least some of the responsibility for the cost of outsourcing a community outreach plan into the joint venture agreement. The private partner often picks up the cost of implementing the community outreach plan until the project is completed. Then the public sector partner assumes responsibility.

Chester, Pennsylvania's Infrastructure Venture

A recent announcement by the city of Chester, Pennsylvania, is a good example of a well-crafted infrastructure joint venture launch. The city's Stormwater Authority produced an attractive one-pager with a picture of an urban garden prominent on the front page over the headline below (with excerpts from the handout):

A New Model For Urban Renewal:
Stormwater Authority of Chester's
Community-Based Public-Private Partnership

The Stormwater Authority of Chester has created a Community-Based Public-Private Partnership (CBP3) to plan, finance, build, and maintain up to $50 million in green stormwater infrastructure over the next 20-30 years on approximately 350 acres to address significant pollution and flooding issues;

improve neighborhood quality of life; assist small, minority-owned businesses; drive economic growth, including significant job creation and cost savings to water and other public and private capital improvement efforts (e.g., streets, housing, economic development, education) in the region.

Here's what you'll want to know about this project:

• US EPA is providing more than $150,000 in technical and planning assistance.

• PENNVEST, Pennsylvania's infrastructure investment authority, has announced a $1 million planning/pre-construction grant.

• The Chester Water Authority has matched the EPA technical and planning assistance funds with a $50,000 grant.

The announcement generated favorable press, including these excerpts from a story that appeared on NextCity.org, an independent global nonprofit news platform for original reporting on urban issues around the world.

Chester, Pennsylvania's recently formed Stormwater Authority announced a partnership that aims to help the city meet a federally mandated sewer system fix while also creating jobs for local contractors and spurring economic development.

The city, which is about 18 miles south of Philadelphia, has a combined sewer-stormwater system ... and has until 2018 to come up with a plan to minimize flooding and eliminate sewage overflow into the Delaware River. They've turned to [a] private company in what the city is calling a "community-based" public-private partnership.

The company ... aims to stick to the "high road infrastructure concept."

Cities' rules around procurement and funding and a lack of collaboration among departments can keep them from realizing all of the potential benefits a single infrastructure project could have. [W]hen departments are required to choose contractors based solely on lowest cost, they may not be able to hire local, even though developing a loyal local workforce could save money in the long-term—and improve economic prospects for the municipality overall.

Horace Strand, executive director of Chester's Stormwater Authority, stress[es] that [the contractor] won't be choosing or developing these ancillary projects, just speeding them along faster than the city might be able to on its own.

"The community drives the mechanism; the community determines what is in their best interest; the community decides what needs to be done," says Strand. "The private partner comes in and asks, 'How can we help you fulfill your vision?'"

And if [the contractor] doesn't meet guidelines agreed to with the city—like a minimum local hire requirement—the company won't get paid.

14 Capital Ideas

When critical, urgent projects lack funding, public-private partnerships are the principal alternative delivery method.

Two questions to answer up front:

1. Can the project be delivered in a safe, efficient, and financially responsible way by engaging with a private sector partner?

2. If so, how?

Costs associated with large projects are usually estimated long before discussions begin about delivery options. Officials will have predetermined how much the project would cost if it were handled in-house. They will also have estimated timelines, resource needs, risk factors, and the costs associated with traditional funding options.

In the past, most large public projects were financed through municipal tax-exempt bonds. If that type of funding is available, it may not be as attractive as it was in the past. Municipal debt costs are based on credit ratings and on an assessment by underwriters of the various risks associated with delivering and maintaining a new public asset.

Most public officials today are employed by government

entities that are struggling with constrained balance sheets, inadequate internal resources, and lower credit ratings than before the Great Recession. Credit ratings will remain under pressure, reflecting the stubborn problem of underfunded pension obligations, deferred maintenance, and crumbling infrastructure. All of these issues make it more difficult for government to obtain attractive municipal bond rates.

And, in the current environment, municipal debt is losing its presumptive edge over the cost of private capital. When it has been used in the past to fund projects, the norm was to award project work to the lowest bidder without taking into account ongoing maintenance. Today, procurements increasingly take into account the ongoing costs of operation and maintenance to make it easier to compare the cost of revenue and the value of risk transfer. Further undermining the advantages of municipal debt have been rumblings in Congress about revisiting the tax exemption, previously regarded as a sacred cow.

Large projects in the past were often cofunded with revenue from federal grants or state budgets. Some of that funding is still available but the amounts have been significantly reduced. There are other federal revenue sources, including Build America Bonds, Private Activity Bonds, and Move America Bonds. Funds in these programs, however, are restricted to very specific types of projects and Congress is scrutinizing them all. This type of funding could be eliminated at any time.

Another funding option is asset recycling—selling off or otherwise monetizing dormant or unnecessary land and facilities. This tactic is sometimes perceived by the public as outright privatization, or a giveaway, when in fact it can be a complex and efficient transaction. The city of Missoula, Montana, used the asset recycling model to swap desirable city-owned property for a development that included a conference center (see Chapter 12). Asset recycling seems to work best for social infrastructure projects and public entities that don't produce revenue.

The creation of any list of private sector funding sources

will be long and diverse. It includes pension funds, insurance companies, banks, investment firms, master limited partnerships, real estate investment trusts, private foundations, and contractor financing. A number of large investment firms have created new pools of capital specifically for people interested in investing in infrastructure projects.

These potential funders by necessity have lately become very competitive. The abundance of capital has created a buyer's marketplace for procurement executives, giving them an edge in negotiating with private sector partners to lock in favorable capital costs.

Any potential private partner offering to provide funding and assume the greater share of risk will insist on thorough and meticulous due diligence. That is good for all parties and it will result in carefully structured long-term agreements in the end. In most procurement documents, bidders are asked to detail the proposed financing options. They will also be asked for information related to financial stability. Careful planning and careful vetting are considered to be the foundation for successful projects. As Surety & Fidelity Association counsel Joanne S. Brooks warns (in Chapter 6), "If something goes wrong, it's going to go wrong on both sides—the work and the financing."

The next step in the decision-making process is to compare what's being offered by potential private sector partners. Outside advisors bring a wealth of knowledge and experience to the table when in the development of specific selection criteria. While this task will have been done much earlier in the process, the value the advisors provide is always obvious when it is time to make the final decision and select a long-term joint venture partner.

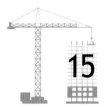

15 Basic Elements of Success

every large public project carries certain degrees of risk, no matter how the project is planned and implemented. Unsuccessful public-private partnerships are almost always the result of overlooked risks that could have been anticipated early in the process or a final contract that is too general in nature.

Occasionally, a governmental entity will select an inexperienced private partner. This usually happens when the evaluation criteria is inadequate or when the procurement process neglects some part of the due diligence, such as in-depth reference checks and rigorous attention to financial stability.

Unseen problems—black swans—are always a risk. A recent large transportation project in Texas fell behind schedule almost as it began because of unanticipated environmental issues and permitting delays. When such incidents happen, it is the private sector partner's financial responsibility, but any delay in a project can result in problems for the public entity. In this case, motorists complained, negative press followed, and work was halted and then restarted, causing safety issues.

An example of a high-visibility problem, from a process

point of view, is the Interstate 69 tollway project in Indiana, described briefly in Chapter 6. It was announced in 2012 as the longest continuous new-terrain interstate construction project in the US, running from Bloomington—home of Indiana University—to Martinsville, about halfway to Indianapolis. Before the contract was signed, the completion date had to be pushed back several times.

The public sector team should have been forewarned when it became clear the award was going to a consortium that had submitted a bid that was $73 million below the next lowest bidder, and $22 million less than the state's internal cost estimate. The public sector team also overlooked the fact that the low bidder, Isolux Corsan, with an 80 percent stake in the project, had no experience building roads and bridges in the US and was having financial problems that were known in the industry.

The Indiana Finance Authority brushed aside requests for a value-for-money analysis and, without explanation, required a performance bond covering only 25 percent of the project's cost. Finally, a state transportation agency employee, the director of maintenance who had no private sector experience or expertise, was hired to oversee the project.

Once underway, construction zones along the route contributed to long commute times and Bloomington city officials labeled the project a safety concern, citing multiple accidents and injuries while work on the road dragged on.

The state of Indiana took the project over in June 2017 but taxpayers have not lost any money and the state will get the new road as planned.

Vetting should never be skipped or incomplete. No engagement can be successful without credible and stable partners. Specific types of experience must be required and cost comparisons must be evaluated. References are indicators of likely success as is the project management expertise being offered.

Other issues to contemplate in the preplanning phase of a project include:

- Contract terms must be absolutely clear in order to avoid disputes later in the project. Both parties must agree to the terms, and the contract should be specific about timelines, success criteria performance benchmarks, responsibilities, and cost accounting.

- Demand projections (such as traffic or other user-related forecasts) can be wrong, and changing circumstances may alter them. Remedies have to be spelled out in the contract. Many troubled engagements have gone bad because of inaccurate demand expectations.

- Transparency is essential. Trust and understanding are impossible without information sharing, progress reports, and agreed-upon operational processes. A project monitor from the public entity should be appointed to oversee the project, a role that must be built into the engagement.

Infrastructure joint ventures and private sector capital are increasingly the only option available to many public entities. These types of partnerships can be abundantly successful with rigorous screening processes and eyes-wide-open management.

Success ultimately falls on the shoulders of government officials. Throughout the process, they are in charge, the stewards of the public's assets, and in control of the outcome.

When it comes to public-private partnerships, the old adage applies: "There are no bad dogs—only bad masters."

Digest

The following material includes excerpts from reports, stories, websites, professional and business associations, and other sources that, all together, give a comprehensive, plain-language overview, details, guidance, best practices, and metrics for anyone contemplating or involved in infrastructure joint ventures of any kind, any size, anywhere.

The complete original documents and materials are readily available on public websites. When available, URL addresses will be found at the end of each entry.

The Digest is divided into the three principal stages common to all infrastructure joint ventures:

PPP Overview—What they are, the types, the structures, and other basic knowledge that will help partners—especially on the public entity side—develop, structure, and evaluate projects that may lend themselves to a public-private partnership.

PPP Financials—How they are funded, by whom, and how are they financially structured, what the risk factors are for both partners, how to compare the financing options, and how to choose the right one for a particular project.

PPP Case Studies—Nothing teaches better than experience, so you will find a series of examples of actual partnerships, a bit of analysis, and details about the outcome or, in some cases, the current stage of the project at the time this book was published. Examples of projects that stumbled on the way to completion are included because we always learn more from mistakes than from successes.

Public officials are encouraged to peruse this material because there is no other option for digging ourselves out of our staggering infrastructure crisis than partnering with private capital. It's a wonder how far ahead of us the rest of the world is considering that public-private partnerships embody all that is best about our system of democratic capitalism.

America is arriving late to the party and we have a lot of catching up to do. It is the goal of this book to provide honest, accurate knowledge that will help public officials and their private partners make the best choices that will produce the best results for the most people.

Readers will find similar material and descriptions from different sources, but each is slightly different. Read it all, or spot read it, or just browse—there's a lot of knowledge, experience, and wisdom for anyone with an interest in rebuilding America.

PPP Overview

The State of US Infrastructure: Backgrounder
by James McBride
Council On Foreign Relations, Oct. 6, 2017
[Excerpts] [Link to original material at the end of this section.]

The $18 trillion U.S. economy relies on a vast network of infrastructure from roads and bridges to freight rail and ports to electrical grids and internet provision. But the systems currently in place were built decades ago, and economists say that delays and rising maintenance costs are holding economic performance back. Civil engineers raise safety concerns as well, warning that many bridges are structurally deficient and that antiquated drinking water and wastewater systems pose risks to public health. Meanwhile, Americans' international peers enjoy more efficient and reliable services, and their public investment in infrastructure is on average nearly double that of the United States.

Debate has intensified over how to improve the nation's infrastructure. Skeptics of federal spending have pushed for new models of private sector involvement, arguing that it is more efficient and cost-effective. Others argue that increased public spending will be necessary to meet the country's growing needs and ensure that development is in the public interest.

Economists argue that robust investment in infrastructure in the twentieth century set the foundation for the nation's strong growth in the aftermath of World War II. Engineer and historian Henry Petroski explains in his book *The Road Taken: The History and Future of America's Infrastructure*, ... delays caused by traffic congestion alone cost the economy over $120 billion per year. ... Some studies have found that delays and avoided trips due to the poor state of the nation's airports cost the economy over $35 billion per year.

Many analysts say that investing in both new infrastructure and current maintenance would positively impact the economy in a number of ways. By increasing efficiency and reliability and lowering transportation costs, it would boost longterm U.S. competitiveness and insulate the economy from shocks. It would also directly add demand and employment, as some fourteen million workers, or 11 percent of the total U.S. labor force, are currently employed in infrastructure-related sectors, according to the Brookings Institution.

A 2014 University of Maryland study found that infrastructure investments added as much as $3 to GDP growth for every dollar spent, with a bigger effect during a recession. Global consulting firm McKinsey estimates that increasing U.S. infrastructure spending by 1 percent of GDP would add 1.5 million jobs to the economy.

In its 2017 report, the American Society of Civil Engineers (ASCE) finds that the nation's infrastructure averages a "D," meaning that conditions are "mostly below standard," exhibiting "significant deterioration," with a "strong risk of failure." The group estimates that there is a total "infrastructure gap" of nearly $1.5 trillion needed by 2025.

According to the DOT, nearly a fifth of all passenger rail lines are in "poor condition." The Environmental Protection Agency estimates that drinking water, wastewater, and irrigation systems will require $632 billion in additional investment over the next decade. Ports and waterways, which handle over one-fourth of the country's freight transport, face mounting delays. The operators of the U.S. electrical grid are struggling to make the necessary investments, and increasing power outages are costing the economy billions of dollars.

The next generation of cell phone and wireless service will require major investments in "small cell" wireless nodes, which are expected to replace traditional cell towers. Quickly advancing drone technology has the potential to revolutionize transportation, disaster response, and delivery services.

A 2017 Brookings report on the state of the nation's internet access finds that a quarter of Americans live in "low subscription" neighborhoods, in which less than 40 percent of residents have access to broadband. Less than 20 percent live in "high subscription" areas with broadband coverage of over 80 percent.

According to the World Economic Forum's Global Competitiveness Report, in 2015 the United States ranked sixteenth in the world in a broad measure of infrastructure quality—down from fifth place in 2002 … behind France, Germany, Japan, and Spain.

Average commuting time in the United States, at forty-eight minutes per day, is well above that of its peers due to congestion and poor public transit. Aviation industry rankings cited by Business Roundtable, a group of American CEOs, put only four US airports in the top fifty worldwide, with the top-ranked coming in at number thirty.

On average, European countries spend the equivalent of 5 percent of GDP on building and maintaining their infrastructure, while the United States spends 2.4 percent. While most European countries fund the bulk of their infrastructure development at the national level, only 25 percent of U.S. public infrastructure funding comes from the federal government. That is down from a peak of 38 percent in 1977, leaving often cash-strapped local governments to bear more of the costs of investment and maintenance.

The federal government supports infrastructure in some indirect ways ... the 1998 Transportation Infrastructure Finance and Innovation Act (TIFIA) provides low interest loans and other credit assistance that local governments can use to finance their infrastructure projects. The federal government also supports the municipal bond market, which is what local governments mostly rely on to finance infrastructure projects.

A small but growing number of infrastructure projects are being organized as joint efforts between government and private developers, known as public-private partnerships. P3s are much more popular in European countries partially because, experts say, the low cost of private financing via municipal bonds in the United States is often an easier and cheaper route for local governments to secure financing.

Many observers argue that the United States will have to find ways to spend significantly more money in order to address its infrastructure deficit. Many economists support raising revenue by increasing user fees, like tolls, or taxes on infrastructure usage. They argue that requiring users to shoulder more of the cost of the nation's infrastructure both raises revenue and encourages more efficient use of resources. At the federal level, the most common proposal is increasing the gas tax.

Cities like New York have considered ... imposing congestion pricing, or fees on cars entering certain parts of the city. New York's 2007 proposal would have reduced car traffic in Manhattan while raising funds that could be spent on upgrading the city's aging transit and other infrastructure. The New York State Assembly never approved the plan, however, and in general such user fees remain politically unpopular in the United States.

Another proposal ... is a national infrastructure bank ... a government-owned corporation like the TIFIA program, would provide cheap, longterm financing for infrastructure projects. Skeptics point out that municipal bonds already offer very cheap financing, especially with interest rates near record lows.

Some economists worry about expanding the federal role ... Others say that onerous regulations and complex approval processes slow down projects and raise costs, and that the federal government should work to reduce them. Meanwhile, other analysts say that the focus on using P3s and relying on private sector financing alone won't address major gaps in the system, such as maintenance of existing roads, bridges, and water lines, since those projects are unlikely to be profitable enough to entice private investors. The United States lacks a culture of private ownership of major infrastructure, which may pose enduring political barriers to efforts to privatize swaths of the transportation system and public utilities.

https://www.cfr.org/backgrounder/
state-us-infrastructure

US PPPs: Issues and Considerations
by Practical Law™ Finance, Thomson Reuters

PPPs are used extensively worldwide but they are not used to the same extent in the US. Most projects in the US are developed using the design-bid-build project delivery mechanism. However, P3s are increasingly being used in the US because of the financial constraints governments are facing.

Private companies have always been involved in the construction of roads and other infrastructure facilities, but their involvement declined in the last 50 years following the implementation of the federal Highway Trust Fund to finance transportation infrastructure projects.

—

Resistance to PPPs in the US

There is a lot of resistance in the US to using PPPs. The reasons for this resistance include concerns that:

- Public assets would be operated by private parties who will not properly maintain them in order to maximize their profits. However, PPP agreements typically have extensive provisions regarding operation and maintenance (O&M). Some of these provisions include:
  - setting out a detailed maintenance and repair schedule;
  - specifying performance standards with which the private sector party must comply and methods for measuring and ensuring compliance;
  - authorizing the right of the public agency to approve the O&M operator selected by the private sector party;
  - establishing an O&M reserve account to ensure that funds are available to make necessary improvements and repairs;
  - authorizing the public agency to audit and inspect the project facilities;

- authorizing the public agency to withhold payments to the private sector party following an event of default or to require payments from the project's end users to be deposited in a segregated account; and
- authorizing the public agency to step in to operate the project and undertake repairs and charge the cost of these repairs to the private sector party (by deducting these amounts from fees owed or applying tolls received from the project's end users depending on the fee structure.

- An asset of national security significance will be controlled by a foreign entity. However, mechanisms are in place to regulate foreign ownership of sensitive US assets.

- Transferring a project's future revenues to the private sector disadvantages taxpayers who no longer benefit from these funds. This criticism can be offset if the public agency:
  - makes an effort to inform the public of the benefits of the project, including the funds it will receive from the private sector party; and
  - conducts a thorough and complete Value for Money (VFM) analysis.

- Using the project will become more expensive (for example, the private sector party will increase tolls). However, PPP agreements typically include extensive provisions regarding user fees. For example, the agreement may:
  - provide that the user fees are fixed for a certain period of time after closing and thereafter subject to adjustments in accordance with the Consumer Price Index, a fixed percentage or other applicable index; or
  - require that any increases be approved by the government or implemented following a public hearing

or a comment period. It should be noted that many project participants resist this approach because of the time it takes and the potential of turning price increases into a political issue.

—

When Should PPPs be Used?

PPPs are not appropriate for all projects. To determine whether a PPP is the best method for procuring a particular infrastructure project, public agencies typically evaluate:

- Whether the proposed project will provide a service or benefit that is best provided by the government. The answer depends in part on the nature and location of the project, the expectations of the public and the political climate in which the public agency operates.
- The capital investment required to build, operate and maintain the project. PPPs are typically appropriate for large-scale projects that involve significant capital investment that may be beyond the public agency's capacity.
- Whether the public agency can afford to forgo the revenues it would receive if it operated the project.
- In the case of PPPs being entered into for asset monetization, the amount of the upfront payment the public agency receives and the uses to which these funds are applied. The fee can be used to retire debt, provide services and invest in other infrastructure projects.
- Whether the public agency has or will have the funds necessary to operate and maintain the project on an ongoing and long-term basis.
- The technical and technological requirements of the project. If these are beyond the expertise of the public agency, it may be better to allocate the design and construction risk to a third party.
- Whether a private sector party may be a more efficient service provider.

- Whether operational controls can be established to monitor the private sector party to ensure that the service is provided properly to the public.
- To assist the public agency in making this evaluation and in determining whether a PPP is a viable option, many public agencies also conduct a value for money analysis.

—

Value for Money (VFM) Analysis

A VFM analysis measures the relative costs of a project if it is procured using traditional public procurement methods versus a PPP to determine the best value for the public agency. It is a comparison of the costs and benefits of traditional government contracting versus the costs and expenses of a PPP structure over the life of the project. This comparison takes into account:

- The net present costs of the project over its entire useful life, including:
  - financing, design, construction and O&M costs; and
  - any payments the public agency may be required to make to the private sector party.
- The risks that would be retained by the public agency, transferred to the private sector party, or shared between the two parties, including:
  - construction costs overruns;
  - higher than expected O&M costs;
  - demand risk (the risk that the public will not use the project to the extent required); and
  - collection risk (the risk that the project's end users will not pay for the service).
- The net present value of the payments the public agency would receive from the private sector party or the project's end users over the life of the project (for example, the fee for entering into the PPP agreement or ongoing royalties) if it operated the project.

- The skills and expertise the private sector party brings to the project.
- The public's ability to pay any user fees that may be required. In some PPP structures, the private sector party obtains third-party loans to finance the performance of its obligations under the PPP agreement. These user fees (taking into account the term of the agreement and a reasonable level of use) are typically calculated to enable the private sector party to repay these loans and other costs.
- Whether in the absence of private sector participation, the project would be developed at all.
- The residual value of the project at the end of the term of the PPP agreement.

—

Types of PPPs

The structure used for any particular project depends on:
- The functions (design, construction, financing, operation and/or maintenance) the private sector party will perform and the risks it will assume.
- Whether the project is a new build or a modification or monetization of an existing facility.
- The degree of operational control the public agency wants to have over any aspect of the project.
- The nature of the project. If the project involves an asset important to national sovereignty or security or a service that is viewed as a core responsibility of the government, the PPP may be structured to allow the private sector party to lease or operate the project but never own it.
- Whether the private sector party will own the project assets at any time during the term of the agreement.
- Whether the project will have any residual value at the end of the agreement.
- The terms of any PPP enabling legislation. Some

legislation specifies the projects that are eligible for the PPP structure and delivery mechanism that can be used.

There are no universally accepted definitions for the terms. Different terms are often used to refer to the same structure depending on the jurisdiction. In many of the structures, the public agency is responsible for financing the project's construction. The scope of the public agency's liability in these structures is generally different. In non-PPP structures ... the public agency is generally responsible for all construction costs including any costs overruns. In addition, the public agency may also have to pay to correct any design or construction defects.

The public agency cannot be sure of its financial exposure. This is especially an issue if the public agency is relying on limited tax revenues or grants. The public agency has a better sense of its financial exposure in a PPP project because the amount it pays to the private sector party to construct the project is typically determined in advance and is generally fixed. If additional funds are required to complete construction, the private sector party is typically required to make up the shortfall.

Design-Build (DB)

This is the most basic of the PPP structures (and the most commonly used in the US) and allocates the fewest obligations and risks to the private sector party. In this structure:

- The private sector party designs and constructs the project for a fixed fee payable by the public agency. Because one party is responsible for design and construction, unlike in the DB structure, there are no issues as to the party who bears the design risk.
- The public agency is responsible for financing but saves the costs and time of entering into separate contracts.
- The public agency owns the asset and is responsible for O&M of the project. The public agency can either enter

into an O&M agreement with a private sector party or do the O&M itself using internal resources.

Design-Build-Finance (DBF)

In this structure, the private sector designs, builds and provides full or partial financing for the construction of the project and the public agency is responsible for the O&M of the project. This structure raises several issues, including:

- Because the private sector has limited responsibility post-closing (for example, warranty obligations for a certain period), it may not take a life-cycle approach to the design and construction of the project.
- The public agency retains the risk of the project's operations, including issues that may arise because of design and construct defects. While the private sector party has warranty obligations, these may not be enough to compensate the private party for the higher O&M costs.

Design-Build-Operate (DBO)

Similar to DB structure, except the private sector party also operates the project. Operating a large-scale project often requires a lot of technical expertise and significant investment in personnel that the public agency may not have. This structure enables the public agency to shift this responsibility to the private sector party. The public agency is responsible for financing the project's construction and maintenance costs.

Design-Build-Maintain (DBM)

This structure is similar to the DB structure, except that the private sector party also maintains the project. The public agency pays an agreed amount for these services and if more funds are required, it is typically the responsibility of the private sector party. Maintenance of the project can be expensive and being able to shift responsibility for repairs to the private sector party can result in significant cost savings to the public agency. In addition, knowing that it will be responsible for maintaining the project may result in the project being built to a higher standard to reduce maintenance costs.

Design-Build-Operate-Maintain (DBOM)

In this structure, the private sector party is responsible for (and bears the risks associated with) the design, construction and O&M of the project. The public agency maintains ownership and is responsible for financing the construction of the project. The private sector party may be paid from the project's end users or the public agency (see Structuring Payments under a PPP Agreement). The advantage of this structure over the DBO and DBM structures is that both operations and maintenance of the project are already provided for. In cases where the public agency is responsible for either or both of these, it may not have the funds available in its annual budget to do so which may cause the project to fall into disrepair.

Design-Build-Finance-Operate (DBFO)

This structure is similar to the DBO structure except that the private sector party is also responsible for financing the project. Title to the project remains with the public agency. The private sector party may be paid by the public agency or from fees collected from the project's end users (see Structuring Payments under a PPP Agreement).

Design-Build-Finance-Operate-Maintain (DBFOM)

Under this structure, the private sector party is responsible for designing, building, financing, operating and maintaining the project for a specified period. The project is owned by the public agency. This structure:

- Allocates the most risk to the private sector party.
- May be the most efficient ... the private sector must take a life-cycle approach to the project to ensure it minimizes the costs of operating and maintaining the project.

The private sector party may be paid by the public agency or from fees collected from the project's end users. If it is paid by the users, the private sector party also bears demand and revenue risk.

Design-Build-Finance-Operate-Maintain-Transfer (DBFOMT)

This structure is similar to the DBFOM model, except that the private sector owns the asset for the term of the PPP agreement after which ownership, operations and maintenance are transferred to the public agency.

Lease, Develop, and Operate

In this model, which is typically used for existing or brownfield projects, the private sector party leases an existing facility from a public agency, invests its own capital to renovate, modernize and/or expand the facility. Then, the private sector party operates and maintains the project under a contract with the public agency. In exchange for assuming these obligations, the private sector party is typically entitled to receive payments from the public for use of the facility. This may be used when vesting title to the assets in the private sector party for any period may be not appropriate or desired.

Concession

In a concession, the public agency sells to a private sector party the right to operate and maintain an existing project for a specified time which can be for as long as 99 years (for example, the $1.8 billion Chicago Skyway project has a concession term of 99 years and the $3.8 billion Indiana Toll Road project has a concession term of 75 years). In exchange for operating and maintaining the project, the private sector party is entitled to receive payments from the end users of the project (for example, tolls). In this structure, the public agency continues to own the project assets and control of the project reverts to it at the end of the concession term.

Structuring Payments Under a PPP Agreement

The payments the private sector party receives for performing its obligations under the agreement may be structured several ways. The payment structure used depends on:

- The party who will assume the demand and collection risks (see Value for Money (VfM) Analysis).
- The amount of the tolls or user fees rates, including whether the public can be required to pay these fees.

The private sector party may be paid:

- A fixed fee by the public agency once the project is ready and available for use (see Availability Based PPPs).
- A variable fee by the public agency based on the public's usage of the facility (see Shadow Toll Based PPPs).
- A fee by the project's end users (see User Fee PPPs).
- A combination of any of the above.

Availability Based PPPs

In this fee structure, the public agency makes payments to the private sector party once the project or facility is available for use (subject to compliance with the agreed performance criteria and standards). The public agency bears the demand and collection risks under this structure because the amount it pays to the private sector party does not change even if the project is not used to the extent anticipated. The public agency may be able to offset the availability fee with user fees received from the public. However, whether or not it actually collects these fees has no effect on its payment obligations to the private sector party. As a result, this fee structure relies (and can impose significant pressure) on the public budget. However, paying availability fees over the life of the project may be preferable to making the capital investment necessary to build the project.

Although demand risk is not an issue for the private sector party, this structure does raise other concerns, including:

- If budget approval is required for the public agency to make the availability payments, is there a risk that such approval may not be given in a timely manner or at all? Is this approval subject to any conditions?

- Is there a likelihood that the public agency may breach its obligations under the agreement? Depending on the location of the project, the private sector party should consider obtaining political risk insurance (see Practice Note, Political Risk Insurance: Is it Necessary?).
- What is the likelihood that the public agency will become unable to pay its debts?
- If the public agency is a government owned entity, are its obligations guaranteed by the government?
- How is availability defined? If the project must be taken out of service because of a force majeure event, for repair or at the request of the public agency, what obligations does the public agency have to make these payments?
- Is the public agency party to any other P3 agreements that require them to make availability payments? The more of these agreements that exists the greater the budget pressure.

Shadow Toll Based PPPs

Typically used for transportation projects, shadow tolls are per vehicle amounts paid to the private sector party by the public agency and not the users of the facility. This is used when it may not be feasible for the road to include toll facilities. The more the road is used, the higher the payments the public agency is required to pay to the private sector party. These payments can, therefore, impose a significant burden on the public agency's finances. To minimize this pressure, many agreements include a cap on the amount the public agency is required to pay. In this structure, the private sector party and the public sector share the demand risk.

The private sector should take steps to ensure that:

- The project is used as expected.
- The government does not construct a competing project

that may reduce demand.
- The government does not adopt legislation (for example, zoning changes) that reduce demand.
- Use of the project can be independently verified.

User Fee PPPs

The end users pay the private sector party for the use of the facility (for example, tolls). As a result, the private sector party bears the demand and collection risks. To mitigate these risks, private sector parties:
- Conduct extensive traffic and other applicable studies to determine the reasonable level of use that can be expected.
- Require the public agency to agree not to build a competing project or implement legislation that may adversely affect demand.
- May require the public agency to guarantee a certain level of use and make payments to the private sector party if such minimum amount is not achieved.
- Include in the PPP agreement extension or renewal provisions to allow the private sector party sufficient time to recoup its investment and earn a return.

https://uk.practicallaw.thomsonreuters.com
Reference 3-504-9995
Practical Law™ Finance
Thomson Reuters [Excerpted]
PPP Basics: Step-by-Step

Public-Private Partnership Facilities and Infrastructure

The following are excerpts from material published on the website of the National Institute of Governmental Purchasing/Institute for Public Procurement, described as "intended as a reference, to be shared with elected public officials, government executives, and private sector executives on the use of and procurement through P3 contracts."

The NIGP is an advocacy organization of procurement professionals founded in 1944 that provides its members with educational and research programs, professional support and development, and technical services. [Find a link to the full document at the end.]

Standard

If considering a P3 contract, the entity should ensure specialized expertise (e.g., finance, real estate, technology) among the team assigned to the project. A certain amount of flexibility must be incorporated into P3 contracts to address how future issues will be approached, including a process for resolution. While the private partner may share in financing the project, the government will always be held responsible for the outcome.

...

A P3 contract allocates risks to the party (the government or the contractor) best able to manage the risks and may assign a higher level of responsibility for means and methods to the private partner.

Elements

Element 1:

P3s include Design (D) and Build (B) elements in a single contract for the construction of public facility or infrastructure projects. ... Adding the component of Maintenance (M) into the same contract increases the complexity of a contract and would be referred to as a "design-build-maintain" (DBM) P3. Operations (O) and Maintenance (M), separately or in combination, do not constitute a P3 unless combined with Design and Build.

...

Some examples of public facility and infrastructure projects that might use a P3 contract are:
- Roads, highways, tunnels, and bridges
- Civic centers and arenas, sports stadiums, recreation sites and facilities
- Water/Wastewater systems
- Industrial parks
- Museums, theaters, libraries
- Housing projects, dormitories, detention centers
- Hotels, conference centers, parking garages
- Communications infrastructure

Element 2:

P3 contracts range from simple to complex along a continuum that includes Design (D), Build (B), Finance (F), Operations (O), and Maintenance (M). Design-Build (DB), the foundation of P3 contracts, features the least number of components with private sector responsibility. As additional components (F, O, M) are added and the contract becomes more complex, the responsibility for means and methods moves toward the private sector.

Element 3:

Contracting principles should reflect the values and mission of the entity. The P3 agreement must provide better value, better quality, or exhibit practical advantages (e.g., access to private sector capital or acceleration of construction timeframes) that cannot be achieved solely by the public sector.
- The decision to use a P3 must be justified by a thorough

analysis of all project delivery alternatives, with a decision process that must include and be transparent to the public.

- Core competencies of the public and private partners must be complementary, thus making the partnership necessary and stronger.
- The contract must include adequate safeguards to protect the public from additional costs or service disruptions in the event of material default or cancellation of the agreement by either party.
- A P3 must not be used to avoid the normal budget process, voter approval, or legislative/governing board approval. If access to private capital is pursued as a means to avoid debt limits or requirements (e.g., voter approval), then public procurement professionals are obligated to raise concerns which, along with justification (who is making the decision and why), should be documented in the public record.

Criteria for choosing a P3 may include:

- Public regulation of operational decisions regarding the use of facilities or infrastructure by a private partner (e.g., for a parking garage, the government would decide what percentage of parking spots are designated for employees versus shoppers).
- Public responsibility for determining the options, including the type of facility and infrastructure, that would best achieve the desired public function outcomes (e.g., library access could be achieved by designing and building one large library or several branches).

Element 4:

A P3 contract follows the procurement cycle and requires a formal plan for each stage. Procurement must use an increased degree of diligence and expertise to find a way to market the opportunity, seek full and open competition, and balance all the risks and responsibilities associated with the project. The formal plan should ensure all elements of the procurement cycle, from need to disposal, are addressed.

—

Element 5:

A feasibility study is the most fundamental and critical factor in the success of the project. The entity is responsible for planning decisions, but determining needs, creating a business case with alternatives, and analyses of the alternatives should follow an open process that includes relevant stakeholders, including potential private sector partners.

The inclusion of the potential private sector partners throughout the feasibility assessment phase is critical. Holding pre-solicitation conversations can provide ample opportunity to transparently share information and prevent any misperceptions surrounding the process with potential partners.

To make an informed decision ... the entity must first assess and justify the need for the project and explain the desired outcome in detail. A description of the challenge or opportunity will provide clear connections between the project objective and possible solutions.

Long-term funding is often the basis, and a primary limiting factor, for the public sector to proceed with major public facility or infrastructure projects. Regardless of how a project is specifically financed, the total cost of the project will ultimately impact the public sector revenue source. During the assessment process, the entity must consider whether the proposed project will garner the necessary public and political support.

An assessment of how Federal, state, and local regulations may affect the contemplated project should be conducted. Some factors that need to be taken into account may include:

- Legislative processes (e.g., whether governing bodies must approve a P3 agreement or award)
- Voter approval (e.g., debt)
- Tolling authorities

- Rate setting requirements for system revenues
- Public ownership
- Restrictions on public debt
- Federal or state financing eligibility
- Tax exemption requirements
- Liability or insurance requirements
- Antitrust statutes
- Public budgeting requirements
- Collective bargaining agreements
- Open meetings and public records laws
- Environmental review

A broad analysis should be conducted during the assessment to identify internal and external factors that may support or endanger the project. A long-term project may be impacted by internal finances, resources, and capacity of the entity. A long-term project may be impacted by external factors, which may include:

- The interests of current politicians weighed against choices that should be left for the future
- Changing interests of special interest groups and the public
- Scrutiny by public and media
- Changing user demographics
- Social impacts
- Shifts in the economy
- New, disruptive technologies
- Force majeure events
- Private partner defaults

Element 6:

A business case should be used to compare, contrast, and explain alternatives to a P3. The business case can be used to outline timing and support budgetary issues and funding. A value for money (VFM) analysis should be conducted and contrasted with a public sector comparator. Early analyses may be updated during the selection and negotiation stages, and be subjected to an impartial review process.

Potential benefits to the use of a P3 contract may include:

- Accelerated project delivery timeframes and improved economic efficiency
- Creation of economic development benefits or social impacts
- Improved quality and savings
- Increased public budget certainty
- Operation and Maintenance components that act as an extended warranty of quality and workmanship
- Improved asset conditions and higher residual values by contracting for Operation and Maintenance
- Increased staff capacity to work on other activities

Potential challenges to the use of a P3 contract may include:

- Offering projects that are of commercial interest to the private sector
- Gathering unified support (e.g., public, elected officials).
- Providing a single public sector voice for negotiations
- Developing realistic assumptions and calculations for long-term contracts and projects that ensure the public investment is fair
- Determining how much flexibility to build into the agreement
- Dealing with complexities that may increase preparation time and transaction costs
- Gathering sufficient supplier references and resources

The private partner in a P3 contract often seeks certainty and advantage. This can lead to less flexibility for the entity than what is typically afforded through traditional procurements. Before moving forward with a P3 contract, the entity must ensure that sufficient staff capacity and expertise are available to manage the contract throughout the planned timeframe. The entity must develop a "Plan B" should the chosen alternative fail at any point.

Element 7: The Solicitation

Once a P3 contract is determined to be feasible: develop a procurement plan with project objectives, success factors, evaluation criteria, procurement steps, and milestones … how to build and issue a solicitation for private partners. Open competition should be promoted whenever possible, recognizing that sometimes limited or no competition is justified.

Defining critical success factors for the entity, the project will be more attractive to the private sector and lead to the selection of the best partner. These factors also will contribute to building public support while complying with the law and affirming values and guiding principles of public procurement.

Procurement should develop a formal communication plan for potential proposers that balances transparency and confidentiality … and impact on competition and on social values.

Considerations may include:

- Should certain project aspects suitable for small to midsized firms be procured separately?
- Should requirements for subcontractor participation be included?
- Do applicable laws allow requirements for subcontractor participation?
- Is there sufficient availability of potential P3 contractors and subcontractors?
- Would an advertising plan attract more competition?
- Is there sufficient time for private partners to organize and respond?

During this phase of the planning process, procurement should:

- Be prepared to respond to public scrutiny and media inquiries.

- Appoint a project team and technical evaluation committee with relevant expertise (e.g., financial, design, real estate) to support the plan.
- Be aware of the political environment and outside pressures that might impact the process.
- Keep the focus on achieving the business objectives of the prospective P3 contract and build relationships with stakeholders and constituencies.
- State the defined public need and desired outcomes.
- Utilize performance-based contracting principles to define requirements and standards that allow potential partners to propose their best approach.
- Be aware of election timelines or budgetary periods that may impact procurement milestones.

The financing packages offered by the proposers are a critical selection factor. An outside financial consultant may be hired to evaluate the packages. The consultant must have no conflicts of interest nor any financial dealings with any of the firms that comprise the potential vehicle. At a minimum, the proposal should:

- Identify each proposed source of financing
- Identify the method of payment preferred by the proposer (e.g., tolls, availability payments)
- Document firm commitments from each source of financing in the solicitation requirements

Element 8: Partner Selection

Selection factors should include complexity of the project, overall risk, and project completion deadlines. An entity may choose to open a P3 dialog with the potential partner through a publicly advertised solicitation requesting information or solutions to the defined challenge. Responses will consist of unpriced proposals or technical solutions that can be used to assist in assessing the feasibility of a project and to determine whether the project should be procured as a P3.

—

When using a Request for Proposals (RFP), the inclusion of qualitative and quantitative evaluation factors will help to ensure the successful selection of a qualified contractor(s). The RFP method should include mandatory requirements that are evaluated on a pass/fail basis.

A Request for Qualifications (RFQu) is a means of prequalifying prospective contractors. The first step uses qualitative factors. The second step uses price. Finally, an evaluation team reviews each response. The top-ranked firms are then invited to respond to either a Request for Proposals (RFP) or an Invitation for Bids (IFB).

"Competitive Dialogue" allows for collaboration between buyers and suppliers, to allow suppliers to offer innovative solutions and ideas. Competitive Dialogue is firmly established in Europe and commonly used in awarding contracts.

Discussions are held with selected suppliers in successive stages until a solution is identified. All participating suppliers are then requested to submit final proposals on the basis of the solution resulting from the competitive dialogue. When using this method, the entity ensures equality of treatment for all participating suppliers. No submission is made available to other proposers.

—

A Joint Solutions Procurement (JSP) is similar to Competitive Dialogue, more commonly used in high dollar, complex projects with a high degree of risk.

Steps in the JSP solicitation method:

1. A Request for Information (RFI) is issued. Suppliers are eligible to participate in subsequent discussions or solicitations.

2. Submissions are evaluated by an evaluation team. Rankings are based on the proposed solution and the ability of the supplier to meet the requirements of the project.

3. A formal Request for Proposals (RFP) is then issued to

the suppliers that have offered acceptable solutions. Negotiations are conducted and best and final offers are requested from suppliers responding to the RFP.

—

Unsolicited proposals are sometimes received. The entity should assess the proposal for feasibility and determine if the project is appropriate for a P3 contract. If the government elects to proceed, the procurement process is initiated. If the unsolicited proposal is accepted, a sole source procurement method may be appropriate.

—

Element 9: Contract Negotiation.

Good negotiations are key for ensuring successful outcomes. With multiple proposers, negotiations prior to best and final offers and selection lead to more completely developed proposals. Negotiations with multiple proposers are considered a best practice.

—

Negotiations should address approval authorities and involvement of other stakeholders. Both parties should agree on the actions to be taken and who will be responsible for particular elements of the agreement. The relationships established during the negotiation phase will be reflected in the development and administration of the contract.

Contract development may include:
- Performance-based contracting principles
- Milestones and key performance indicators
- Strong maintenance and safety standards

Public satisfaction measures may be used to trigger changes to operational procedures. Processes for ensuring high quality should include:
- The identification of risk and who will manage the financial burden of cost overruns and delays
- Accountability metrics
- Accommodations for changes in public needs

- Ability to adjust the project to changing conditions
- Language that allows for a high level of openness and communication
- Language that outlines the process and resolution in the event of unexpected events
- A communications plan for informing stakeholders.
- An extensive risk management plan
- Updated economic assumptions that may affect the project outcome
- Provisions for reporting on progress and documenting key decisions by the contractor
- Joint decision making process to be implemented during the project
- How savings will be accrued and distributed
- Contract transition and close out

—

Payments

Contractor payments usually involve one or more of the following:

- Tolls or fees collected directly by the private partner from users of the facility or infrastructure. Tolls should be explained and the contract should ensure that the government either has sole discretion over the establishment and increase of fees, or has final approval of fee increases proposed by the partner.
- Availability or periodic payments (e.g., monthly lump sum payments) made by the government to the private sector partner when the facility or infrastructure is open and available for use. The source of funding for availability payments may come from monies paid by users directly to the government or from other sources.
- Bonus payments or fines tied to key performance indicators.
- Provisions to adjust or renegotiate payments to the private partner.

- Established maximum payments.

Contractor (private partner) payment guarantees should be calculated against the total price paid and align with public need, usage, and sources of revenue.

Following the award of a P3 contract, the contract administration team conducts progress meetings and administers the payment schedule, performance milestones, key performance indicators, change management, dispute elevation, and risk mitigation. The procurement cycle includes assessments that occur throughout the project and help to refine current or upcoming project phases. Lessons learned on one project should be internalized and applied to future procurements.

© 2016 CIPS and NIGP
http://www.nigp.org/docs/default-source/New-Site/
public-private-partnership-(p3)-facilities-and-infrastructure

P3 Fairness Stipends For Losing Bidders
From the Best Practices Guide of AIAI
The Association for the Improvement
of American Infrastructure

When assessing the complexity and scale of public infrastructure projects, the authors of an effective P3 program may consider the cost commitments incurred by private respondents (bidders) during the procurement process. A proposed P3 bill can allow for stipends, which are often viewed as indicative of relative commitment of the procuring authority.

Fairness Stipends: Terms and conditions under which a stipend would be authorized. The responsible public entity should be authorized to pay a stipend to an unsuccessful bidder or proposer that has reached the pre-qualified bidder stage.

Summary:

There are high costs and risks for private sector participants when they respond to a public sector request for qualifications (RFQ) or requests for proposals (RFP) to deliver a capital project using a P3 structure. Stipends are a means to offset some of these costs, essentially one-time payments for work that are often referred to as Payment for Work Products (PFWP). Offering a stipend is a method for the public entity to acquire documents and materials—the intellectual property—that was prepared by respondents to an RFP.

Process:

During the RFQ|RFP process to select a development partner to deliver a capital project using a P3, a public entity will typically receive one-half dozen proposals that respond to the initial qualifications request, the RFQ. After evaluating responses to the RFQ, it is normally the case that up to four prospective development partners will be selected to respond to the follow-on phase of the procurement, the RFP.

Being selected to respond to an RFP is a significant accomplishment and milestone for private sector participants in the procurement process. It is also an invitation to expend significant time, resources and money pursuing business that has a high degree of risk associated with it if they are not the team selected to deliver the project. Prior to responding, private sector teams will perform analyses that evaluate the risks, the likelihood of success, the costs associated with achieving success and if it is worth that investment.

In an initial solicitation, a stipend or one-time payment from the public sector entity may be paid to each of the unsuccessful teams that respond to and completes the requirements of the RFP. The initial solicitation should also indicate the amount of the payment and the requirements for eligibility.

Intellectual Property

In order for the respondents to receive the stipend, it is suggested that the documents and materials prepared by respondents in response to the RFP become the property of the public entity. Intellectual property, including technical studies that are specific to a proposed project or work product that is unique to a site, is a key component of stipends and helps avoid issues and questions that may arise regarding the selective use of public funds.

Therefore, the public entity must understand what information it needs to assess submittals, and how the responses submitted for consideration to the RFP will be evaluated, judged and scored. The public entity will want to understand how and at what cost the information they require is generated and what documents and materials each team will need to produce to provide them with that information.

It is important that the public entity not ask for more information than is necessary to evaluate and score proposals. Understanding the necessary costs to prepare documents and materials will assist in the determination of evaluation and scoring criteria and inform the amount of any stipend offered. Keeping costs of preparing documents and materials to a reasonable amount and offering what the public entity can afford, will also keep the highest quality and most creative respondents engaged.

For the timing of the payment and the delivery of the work product, the public entity should allow selected respondents the opportunity to incorporate alternative technical concepts or good ideas prior to financial close. In most cases, the respondents' submittals provide that their cost of responding to the RFP phase be included as part of their total project compensation, should they be selected to deliver the project.

Should a project not go forward for any reason, or if the project goes partially forward and is then terminated or suspended, the successful bidder should be compensated for costs on the same basis as the unsuccessful competitors, as well as for documented third-party costs for work completed up to the notice of termination or suspension.

Amount:

There is no standard or formula established for determining stipend amounts. On average, the amounts allocated for stipends and paid out (expressed as a percentage of the contract value) range from:

- 0.10 - 0.15% for projects in excess of $1 billion
- 0.25% for projects above $500 million (but smaller than $1 billion)
- 0.4% for projects larger than $250 million; and
- approximately 0.5% for projects larger than $100 million but less than $250 million.

If a procurement is canceled after selection, but prior to financial close, the selected bidder should also receive a payment for work product. Consideration should be given to make this higher than what is given to the losing bidders to compensate them for their winning position and costs expended to reach commercial and financial close. It is important to be clear on what a compliant bid entails. Details should be in the agreement.

Larger projects may require only a partial or interim submission in response to a tiered RFP. This phased procurement approach can limit the amount of the stipend paid to the teams that are not selected. The risk is limited to a stipend for the cost of the work the team that is selected expends on the more detailed submittals.

Conclusion: Stipends, or one-time payments for work product, are an accepted means of off-setting some of these costs and risks and keeping these teams engaged in the procurement process.

Rural Infrastructure and the Role of P3s
Bipartisan Policy Center
By Jake Varn
Thursday, February 23, 2017

Infrastructure proposals for the United States on Capitol Hill are raising concerns that that P3-focused solutions may leave rural communities out in the cold. Rural communities face unique infrastructure needs and significant funding challenges, but P3 projects can be part of the solution. As members of the newly announced Coalition to Modernize American Infrastructure advise, P3s are an "additional tool in the toolbox," one that must be paired with robust federal funding and streamlining reforms.

In all types of communities, both internationally and around the United States, P3s have successfully leveraged private capital and improved project delivery. However, P3s alone are not the answer to our nation's infrastructure funding and financing gap and will not be appropriate for every project.

Unfortunately, P3s have become synonymous with toll roads, a generalization that has persisted over the years. While there are several high-profile toll roads that exist as a result of a P3, in the United States alone, P3s have been used to deliver water treatment plants, broadband systems, rail lines, courthouses, bridges, tunnels, port facilities, and more.

Many assume that if an infrastructure project does not have an upfront user fee, such as tolls, it is impossible to utilize a P3 model. [R]ural areas that for a number of reasons cannot toll a road often feel left out of any P3-focused proposal. However, user fees are just one of many ways that these partnerships can be funded. With the promise of delivering a combination of either higher quality, lower cost, or faster delivery, P3s can be structured to rely on future payments (from either federal, state, or local sources), asset leases or sales, and other innovative sources of revenue, rather than just user fees.

There are several successful P3 projects that are either already operating or are under construction in rural communities across America:

State Route 35, which connects West Virginia to I-64 in southern Ohio, is currently under construction through a P3 agreement.

Virginia is also using a toll-free P3 approach to design and build an interchange and road extension in Lynchburg, to connect the Lynchburg Expressway and U.S. Route 29/460.

Rural communities often suffer from an inability to leverage an economy of scale. It is cheaper to buy a thousand pens once than it is to buy one pen a thousand times. P3s can offer an innovative solution to this challenge, by taking a small project that may not normally attract private investment and bundling it with dozens or even hundreds of similar projects.

In 2013, Pennsylvania bundled the repair of 558 small bridges into a single project and partnered with the private sector to design, build, finance, and maintain each bridge for the next 25 years. Pennsylvania's Department of Transportation estimates that if they repaired these rural bridges under the standard process it would take 13 years longer, cost 30 percent more to build, and cost 20 percent more to maintain.

Outside of transportation, P3s have also been successfully applied in rural water and broadband projects, The city of Holyoke, MA, with a population of 40,000 people, used a P3 agreement to address a sewer overflow problem—millions of gallons of wastewater being discharged into the Connecticut River every year. The project agreement included the construction, operation, and maintenance of a new combined sewer overflow abatement facility and collection systems.

Like many states with large rural populations, Kentucky struggles to provide broadband access. To address this, the state entered a P3 agreement and is in the process of creating a high-speed broadband network that is directly prioritizing rural communities.

In addition to these state and locally driven rural projects, the U.S. Department of Agriculture (USDA) has an agreement with CoBank and Capitol Peak Asset Management to run the U.S. Rural Infrastructure Opportunity Fund to serve as a new source of capital for rural infrastructure projects (including social infrastructure assets like housing and health services). This USDA-led fund has facilitated an investment of $161 million in private capital since 2015 and the partner, CoBank, has lent more than $3 billion in financing to over 400 rural power, water, and community projects.

Despite the wide variety of projects and the option to bundle smaller projects together, the P3 model is not a one-size-fits-all solution. Especially in rural communities, there are specific projects and infrastructure needs where a P3 may not be optimal. However, a more robust P3 approach could also indirectly help address these needs. As states bring more private capital into other infrastructure projects, state funds can be freed up for more traditional projects.

https://bipartisanpolicy.org/blog/
rural-infrastructure-and-the-role-of-p3s/

Insights From PPP Veteran Canada

Canada has had a two-decade head start with public private partnerships and it has amassed a valuable resource library based on the experience of more than 200 infrastructure joint ventures, all of it available online. Any research into whether to consider and how to execute a P3 has to include browsing Canada's extensive P3 Resource Library. The link will be found at the end of this section.

PPP Canada material includes an interactive project map of the country, showing principle infrastructure joint ventures, including brownfield redevelopment, national highways, green energy, local roads, public transit, regional and local airport infrastructure, and waste water infrastructure.

The resource section of the website also includes complete detailed actual value for money analyses for completed projects. You can see what the projection was versus the outcome. These resources are basic roadmaps for those public participants and joint venture groups that are beginning the process of deciding when and where a public private partnership is appropriate, efficient, and realistic.

Some excerpts from the extensive material available follow.

—

Public–private partnerships (P3s) are a long-term performance-based approach to procuring public infrastructure.

- Governments do not pay for the asset until it is built and operational;
- A substantial portion of the cost is paid over the life of the asset and only if it is properly maintained and performs according to specifications; and
- Costs are known upfront and span the life-cycle of the asset, meaning that taxpayers are not on the financial hook for cost overruns, delays or any performance issues over the asset's life.

P3s work because they engage the expertise and innovation of the private sector and the discipline and incentives of capital markets to deliver public infrastructure projects.

P3s transfer a major share of the risk associated with infrastructure development (such as the costs associated with overruns, schedule delays, unexpected maintenance, and/or latent defects in the assets) to the private sector. This is accomplished by engaging the private sector in a bundled contract for the life of the asset. This contract connects ongoing operations and/or maintenance payments to the quality of the original construction.

While they are not the right solution in every case, P3s can provide many benefits when applied to the right projects. Visit our project map to find out more about the P3 projects PPP Canada has facilitated across the country.

—

When Is A P3 The Right Choice?

Public private partnerships are the right solution when the benefits exceed the cost. That requires a thorough value for money analysis. Our experience demonstrates that this upfront work produces better projects even if a P3 approach is not the preferred option, as it requires a more systematic consideration of costs, risks, and performance expectations.

—

A value for money analysis is the comparison between the total project costs (capital base costs, financing costs, retained risks and ancillary costs), at the same point in time for a traditionally delivered project (known as the public sector comparator), and delivery of the same project using the P3 model (known as the shadow bid).

The incremental difference between the public sector comparator and the shadow bid is referred to as the value for money. If the shadow bid costs are lower than the public sector comparator, the P3 project is found to deliver positive value for money to the taxpayer.

Adopting a whole life-cycle approach: The private sector assumes responsibility for all or many of the phases of an asset's life-cycle. In doing so, the private sector assumes the interface risk between the phases, is fully accountable for whether the asset delivers, and is incented to produce the most effective result over the lifespan of the asset. The all-too-familiar problems of poor design, sub-standard construction or inadequate or deferred maintenance become the responsibility of the private sector.

—

The private sector is paid only on performance. In the majority of our projects no payment is made until substantial completion, and a significant portion is paid only over the life of the asset based on clear performance criteria. This aligns financial incentives for on-time, on-budget delivery and for the achievement of performance standards during the useful life of the asset.

Since payments are made only on performance, the private sector partner must raise significant financing for the construction of the asset. Lenders and equity participants provide a level of due diligence and oversight that brings enormous discipline to the process.

In a P3, the public sector specifies the what, not the how, and leaves as much scope as possible to the private sector to develop the best solution to deliver results. Successful P3s tend to be large, complex projects that transfer the risks of some, or all, of the components of the project (design, build, finance, operation and/or maintenance) to the private sector and deliver positive Value for Money.

—

The P3 model is appropriate under these conditions:
- You have a major project, requiring effective risk management throughout the life-cycle;
- There is an opportunity to leverage private sector expertise;

- The structure of the project could allow the public sector to define its performance needs as outputs/outcomes that can be contracted for in a way that ensures the delivery of the infrastructure in the long term;
- The risk allocation between the public and private sectors can be clearly identified and contractually assigned;
- The value of the project is sufficiently large to ensure that procurement costs are not disproportionate;
- The technology and other aspects of the project are proven and not susceptible to short-term obsolescence; and
- The planning horizons are long-term, with assets intended to be used over long periods and are capable of being financed on a lifecycle basis.

—

In a P3, project risks are transferred to the party best able to manage them. By making the private sector responsible for managing more risk, governments reduce their own financial burden. The private sector bids a fixed price for the bundled contract, and must pay out of pocket should any unforeseen expenses arise—cost escalation, construction defects, unexpected maintenance requirements, etc.

—

The private sector is interested in P3s because, as compared to traditional procurement, P3 projects provide the private sector with a greater role in the design, building, financing, and/or operation of public infrastructure and offer a unique business opportunity, allowing private companies to deliver a broad range of services in different industrial sectors over a long term concession period (typically 20 to 30 years). They provide an opportunity to work with stable, bankable partners in governments, and they provide a long-term revenue stream.

http://www.p3canada.ca/en/about-p3s/p3-resource-library/

Public-Private Partnerships and Effective Governing Boards
By Darryl G. Greer and Michael W. Klein
Trusteeship Magazine, May/June 2016
Published by The Association of Governing Boards of Universities and Colleges (AGB)

Risk assessment is the fundamental purpose of trusteeship—to preserve the integrity of an institution and provide guidance in fulfilling its mission. One way is by building public-private partnerships with businesses and other constituencies outside of higher education.

Any successful partnership requires explicit agreement on goals, a commitment to shared responsibilities, and transparent communications. And all public-private partnerships must, in the final analysis, serve the mission of the institution.

—

Enterprise risk management (ERM) should be at the heart of what governing boards do. ... In the final analysis, the whole should be greater than the sum of the parts, one in which the focus on the big picture ... connects with sustaining public trust.

—

The model by which we finance American higher education is rapidly changing from one characterized by public financing as a public good to one that is privately funded from tuition and user fees and supplemented with revenue from noneducational business income. Expectations for greater accountability for college value and outcomes stem from students paying an ever-increasing share of educational cost at public institutions, a diminishing proportion of college revenue from state appropriations, and increasing student and family indebtedness.

Universities must grapple, too, with other tests to support their educational and service missions. These trends have created an era of enterprise for all institutions, one in which new revenue streams ... must be found by building partnerships with businesses and other constituencies outside of higher education.

—

Entering into new partnerships with private and nonprofit organizations has often required colleges to create their own entities, beyond those that already exist, to take advantage of the new flexibility. These organizations, usually created as non-profits, typically are governed by a board of directors, separate from the board of trustees, but often overlapping with constituent members of the institution. In many cases, these members include president, vice president for finance, chief development officer, trustee and foundation representatives, students, and community members.

These new organizations and partnerships require a governing board to take greater responsibility in assessing risk and more responsibility for evaluating how these structures and partnerships support and advance the institution's mission.

A 2009 Association of Governing Boards of Universities and Colleges report, "The State of Enterprise Risk Management at Colleges and Universities Today," found that 60 percent of trustees surveyed said their colleges do not use comprehensive, strategic risk assessment to identify risks to mission success, and that less than half of respondents agreed that senior administrators and board members actively engage in discussion of institutional risk.

—

Boards of trustees should:
- Place risk management at the center of board decision making;
- Ensure senior management is committed to ongoing risk assessment;
- Make certain that someone other than the president is assigned central responsibility for risk management;
- Reinforce the benefit throughout the institution;

- Ensure proper board and staff training;
- Establish human resources policy to reward effective risk management;
- Focus risk management processes on opportunities as well as potential problems; and
- Integrate risk management into the internal audit function, then monitor and evaluate its application.

—

Boards and presidents are cautioned to avoid some common obstacles to effective risk management, as suggested by the accounting and consulting firm Grant Thornton, LLP:

- Viewing ERM as a project rather than an ongoing process;
- Failing to use ERM as a means of setting priorities, getting bogged down attempting to identify all possible risks;
- Creating processes to go around risk management for the sake of comfort or convenience;
- Failing to properly identify the intensity of and long-term versus short-term nature of certain risks; and
- Inability to evaluate risks because of absence or inappropriate use of risk indicators.

Usually a PPP provides innovative means of contracting. The private entity performs functions often associated with a public agency to serve a public purpose, but the public partner remains accountable for the facility or service provided.

Such is the case with colleges, which often create an affiliated body with nonprofit status, and may involve a quasi-public facilitating agency, in addition to contracting with a private company to renovate, construct, operate, maintain, or manage a facility or system. Types of PPP contractual arrangements include design-build, construction manager at risk, build-own-transfer, and lease back.

Under a typical PPP, a university leases property to a

developer, which finances the project with its own equity or with corporate debt. After the facility is constructed to the institution's specifications, the developer usually handles the maintenance of the facility. The developer recovers its costs through room fees.

For example, Montclair State University in New Jersey built a 2,000-bed facility called The Heights in 2012 through a public-private partnership with Capstone Development Partners, which financed the $211 million project with tax-exempt bonds.

The University of Kentucky transferred control of about 6,000 campus beds and apartments to Education Realty Trust in 2012. The university receives ground-lease payments. In exchange, Education Realty collects rent payments from students, and it will also spend up to $500 million to upgrade and construct new dorms, providing more than 2,500 beds in the next few years.

Public-private partnerships help to finance and construct redevelopment projects. Mixed-use facilities connecting colleges to their towns benefit local businesses and residents as well as students, faculty, and college staff. For example, Kent State University is partnering with the city of Kent, Ohio, and private developers on a $110 million, 500,000 square-foot project that includes facilities for the university, such as a building for its College of Architecture and Environmental Design; retail and office space; and a transit center. The College of New Jersey's Campus Town and Rowan University's Rowan Boulevard are two mixed-use PPP success stories in New Jersey.

A key distinction of a PPP from traditional asset development-management schemes is mutual sharing of risks, and in the case of the college, shifting some of the risk burden for performance from the institution to the private sector. Accordingly, important considerations for boards of trustees are the primary purposes served by the partnership, the incentives provided to the private partner, and a thorough understanding of how risks will be shared and assessed.

A PPP proposal from Ohio State University in February 2015 reflects the types of risks at stake. Ohio State proposed a 50-year concession and lease regarding its energy systems, with four components for the private partner: (1) operate and maintain the utility system on the Columbus campus; (2) procure the energy supply for the Columbus campus; (3) achieve energy savings goals, including energy conservation measures; and (4) develop an affinity relationship with Ohio State, including research collaboration with faculty, scholarships and internships for students, and integrated co branded energy marketing opportunities.

The private partner risked a 50-year investment in exchange for an anticipated long-term, predictable cash flow, with new facilities for health sciences, student housing, and athletics scheduled over the next 10 years. The university risked the certainty it had in short-term contracts for electricity in exchange for a substantial upfront payment and a new compensation structure under proposed rate-setting mechanisms with the private partner.

—

Principles of Good Practice and Issues to Avoid

Even though a PPP may provide significant benefit, some principles suggested by Hanover Research and the National Conference of State Legislatures require careful consideration:

- Keep the mission-related purpose in focus.
- Stay informed and make decisions on a factual basis.
- Continually assess the public interest.
- Define success in the long term.
- Involve and educate stakeholders.
- Make the purpose drive the means, not the other way around.
- Make sure that the partnership approach is superior to the traditional one.
- Be clear about financial means and outcomes.

- Be sure not to cut corners in meeting existing requirements of law, regulation, and labor agreements.

—

Questions Boards Should Ask
- How are affiliated organizations structured …what is the makeup of directors? How are they appointed?
- Does it meet standards of transparency?
- How is it accountable to the board of trustees and public?
- How often are the body's mission and bylaws reviewed by the trustees?
- Is the organization's work included in the college or university's ERM processes, and do the trustees receive regular reports on risks associated with the affiliated body?
- What controls are in place regarding legal representation and indemnification?

—

As institutions of higher education act more entrepreneurially, they will seek more creative—and risky—ways to raise revenue through expanded partnerships. In managing risks, trustees … must find new ways to keep focus on paramount issues of transparency and accountability and maintain the public trust.

https://www.agb.org/trusteeship/2016/mayjune/risk-taking-public-private-partnerships-and-effective-governing-boards

7 Keys To Successful P3s

The National Council For Public-Private Partnerships (NCPPP.Org) is a nonprofit advocacy group founded in 1985 that provides extensive knowledge, guidance, expertise, and assistance in enabling and forming public-private partnerships at all levels of government. Its staff and contributors come from both the private and public sectors.

The organization posts excellent material on its website from members and other sources, including "7 Keys to Successful P3s."

According to NCPPP, "The methodology for implementation of P3s can vary, depending on the nature of a given project and local concerns. Given this, it is the position of the NCPPP that these are 'best practices'."

1) Public Sector Champion:

Recognized public figures should serve as the spokespersons and advocates for the project and the use of a P3. Well-informed champions can play a critical role in minimizing misperceptions about the value to the public of an effectively developed P3.

2) Statutory Environment:

There should be a statutory foundation for the implementation of each partnership. Transparency and a competitive proposal process should be delineated in this statute. However, unsolicited proposals can be a positive catalyst for initiating creative, innovative approaches to addressing specific public sector needs.

3) Public Sector's Organized Structure:

The public sector should have a dedicated team for P3

projects or programs. This unit should be involved from conceptualization to negotiation, through final monitoring of the execution of the partnership. This unit should develop Requests For Proposals (RFPs) that include performance goals, not design specifications. Consideration of proposals should be based on best value, not lowest prices. Thorough, inclusive value for money (VFM) calculations provide a powerful tool for evaluating overall economic value.

4) Detailed Contract (Business Plan):

A P3 is a contractual relationship between the public and private sectors for the execution of a project or service. This contract should include a detailed description of the responsibilities, risks and benefits of both the public and private partners. Such an agreement will increase the probability of success of the partnership. Realizing that all contingencies cannot be foreseen, a good contract will include a clearly defined method of dispute resolution.

5) Clearly Defined Revenue Stream:

While the private partner may provide a portion or all of the funding for capital improvements, there must be an identifiable revenue stream sufficient to retire this investment and provide an acceptable rate of return over the term of the partnership. The income stream can be generated by a variety and combination of sources (fees, tolls, availability payments, shadow tolls, tax increment financing, commercial use of underutilized assets or a wide range of additional options), but must be reasonably assured for the length of the partnership's investment period.

6) Stakeholder Support:

More people will be affected by a partnership than just the public officials and the private sector partner. Affected employees, the portions of the public receiving the service, the press, appropriate labor unions and relevant interest groups will all have opinions, and may have misconceptions about a partnership and its value to all the public. It is important to communicate openly and candidly with these stakeholders to minimize potential resistance to establishing a partnership.

7) Pick Your Partners Carefully:

The "best value" (not always lowest price) in a partnership is critical in maintaining the long-term relationship that is central to a successful partnership. A candidate's experience in the specific area of partnerships being considered is an important factor in identifying the right partner. Equally, the financial capacity of the private partner should be considered in the final selection process.

—

https://www.ncppp.org/ppp-basics/7-keys/

Federal P3 Value for Money Analysis
US Federal Highway Administration Factsheet:
P3 Toolkit

For highway projects, a private partner may participate in some combination of design, construction, financing, operations, and maintenance, including the collection of toll revenues. A Value for Money (VFM) analysis is used to compare the financial impacts of a P3 project against those for the traditional public delivery alternative. The methodology for carrying out a VfM analysis involves:

- Creating a Public Sector Comparator (PSC), which estimates the whole-life cost of carrying out the project through a traditional approach.
- Estimating the whole-life cost of the P3 alternative (either as proposed by a private bidder or a hypothetical "shadow bid" at the pre-procurement stage).
- Completing an apples-to-apples comparison of the two approaches.

———

The Public Sector Comparator (PSC) estimates the hypothetical risk-adjusted cost if a project were to be financed, built, and operated by the public sector using its traditional procurement approach. It includes the baseline PSC cost, ancillary costs, financing costs, retained risk, transferable risk, and competitive neutrality.

- The baseline PSC includes all capital and operating costs associated with building, owning, maintaining, and delivering the service over the pre-determined period of time.
- Ancillary costs include right-of-way and procurement.
- Financing costs are those associated with interest on public debt and issuance fees.
- Retained risk refers to the value of any risk that is not transferable to the bidder, and transferable risk refers to

the value of any risk that is transferable to the bidder.
- Competitive neutrality adjustments remove any competitive advantages and disadvantages that accrue to a public agency by virtue of its public ownership, such as its freedom from taxes.
- The present value of forecasted toll revenue is generally subtracted from total PSC costs to get net present cost.

—

The cost elements of a P3 option are:
- The present value of payments to be made to the private partner, which account for transferred risks and nancing costs
- The value of any risks retained by the public sector
- Any ancillary costs borne by the public agency

At the pre-procurement stage, a shadow bid is constructed to estimate what the private sector would bid in response to a P3 request for proposals.

Public Sector Comparator vs. P3 Option

Generally, a P3 proposal must cost less than the PSC to be preferable to traditional procurement; however, even if P3 costs are higher, qualitative factors not included in the quantitative analysis may still make the P3 approach preferable.

When a P3 presents overall savings, it is said to provide "value for money." This value is usually expressed as the percent difference by which the PSC cost exceeds the P3 cost. Small changes in the assumptions underlying the analysis can tip the balance; thus, it is important to undertake a sensitivity analysis to understand the critical assumptions.

Example Of A Value For Money Analysis

An is the comparison between a public procurement with a baseline present cost of $60 million and a P3 shadow bid for which the baseline present cost (net of financing costs) is $65 million.

Although the baseline P3 cost is $5 million more and imposes an additional $6 million in ancillary and financing costs, thereis a $13-million reduction in the cost of risk due to transfer of some risks to the private sector and $8 million in competitive neutrality adjustments overcome these cost differences and result in a net savings to the Government of $9 million overall, offering 8% in value for money.

This example illustrates the central trade-offs that often characterize P3 procurement: The Government trades away significant risks in exchange for higher baseline costs and financing costs in the P3 scenario.

http://www.fhwa.dot.gov/ipd/forum/vfm_for_ppps/index.htm

PPP FINANCIALS

Bundling: A Growing Trend
As Stakeholders Look to Unlock
Potential of the Infrastructure Asset Class
S&P Global Ratings, Jan. 31, 2017
By Trevor d'Olier-Lees, Winston Chang,
and Kurt Forsgren

In the ongoing debate over the need for global infrastructure investment, the focus generally falls on the financing gap. Huge numbers make for great headlines, (but) this big-picture discourse often falls short of discussing practical, real-world approaches to the problem.

Bundling of infrastructure assets is gaining momentum, driven by the needs of diverse groups of stakeholders. This includes governments and constituents, institutional investors, and vendors. Widespread use of bundling in the private sector has led to growing interest in bundled P3 opportunities.

There is a wide range of bundling approaches and the market continues to create new structures as new asset classes emerge and governments and/or multilateral agencies look for solutions to fund smaller assets or support new markets. The concept of asset bundling is not new. There have been instances where governments have packaged assets into a single financing to meet scale requirements or to improve credit strengths by attracting larger, more experienced contractors.

While bundling can complicate the credit analysis of a transaction, we've observed that it can also, when executed, lead to the opening of new sources of capital for infrastructure. An example of this approach is the Penn Bridges project

(Plenary Walsh Keystone Partners LLC), in which Pennsylvania's Department of Transportation (PennDOT) bundled 558 bridges.

The state Office of Policy & Public-Private Partnerships said the decision for a P3 approach was to:

- Replace structurally deficient bridges more quickly;
- Standardize design and construction;
- Provide better value to taxpayers;
- Provide economy-of-scale savings and lower life-cycle costs; and
- Free up dollars for other projects.

Scale is an important factor in achieving cost-efficient financing of construction and/or operations because infrastructure is so capital-intensive by nature. One infrastructure asset type that we think might attract bundling structures in the future is the U.S. water industry, still largely decentralized with more than 50,000 authorities with infrastructure more than 50 years old. We've observed that interest in bundling water assets is being expressed in other countries.

Individual renewable energy projects also tend to be fairly small. Bundling is a strategy that governments and sponsors turn to so as to achieve more efficient or alternative forms of financing. For example, an industry group in the US (Solar Access to Public Capital, SAPC) was convened by National Renewable Energy Laboratory with the goal of accelerating the solar photovoltaic (PV) industry's access to public capital through securitized instruments and other investment vehicles. There have been a number of rooftop solar securitization financings we've rated in the US that have generated interest in similar approaches by sponsors in other parts of the world.

—

Use of known proven technology generally supports quicker analysis and is a credit benefit under our methodologies. The use of experienced contractors with stronger balance sheets in the context of a design and build contract used in P3 is usually a credit positive for S&P Global Ratings. Similarly, this approach has the potential to support stakeholder goals of faster construction delivery and cost savings, as was observed in the Penn Bridges example mentioned above.

On the other hand, a diverse bundle of complex heterogeneous technologies could have a portfolio benefit of diversity but the task of analyzing the transaction becomes time-consuming, challenging, and with greater uncertainty as it relates to potential credit benefit.

We expect to see an evolution in approaches to bundling structures.

—

[I]n the evaluation of a bundled bridge project, we observed that a systematic approach to our analysis was possible given a number of factors that included:

- The selection of the type of bridges allow for the independent engineer to bucket them into three types of similar risk profiles. The bridges used proven technology, with no unusual technical challenges with respect to the design and construction of bridge structures.
- Given there were multiple bridges, this meant multiple geotechnical risks to be considered. However, site specific information was supplied at each of the bridge locations including subsurface information available for each bridge abutment and pier location. There was also compensation under the concession for relief events such as for mines, archaeological remains, and unforeseen utilities. Given the relatively high level of information, the geotechnical risk was considered low by independent engineers.

https://www.spglobal.com/our-insights/Bundling-a-Growing-Trend-as-Stakeholders-Look-to-Unlock-the-Potential-of-the-Infrastructure-Asset-Class.html

Infrastructure Finance FAQs
Bipartisan Policy Center, Jan. 6, 2017
By Sarah Kline, Fellow

Making sense of the many infrastructure financing ideas currently being discussed can be confusing. Many distinct funding and financing options are lumped together under the finance heading, when in fact they are different mechanisms that will yield different results.

Some examples of financing proposals include tax credits, public-private partnerships, private activity bonds, and a national infrastructure bank. These proposals differ from the traditional approach the federal government has taken, which is to provide state and local communities with direct funding (i.e., grant dollars) targeted to a particular infrastructure sector such as highways or water.

To craft an infrastructure package that meets America's broad needs, policymakers will have to determine the appropriate balance between funding and financing and choose from among the various ways to accomplish each. These FAQs are intended to provide a basic overview of key concepts in infrastructure finance.

To craft a package that meets America's needs, policymakers will have to determine the right balance between funding and financing.

Q: What's the difference between funding and financing?

A: When it comes to federal support for infrastructure, there is an important distinction between funding and financing.

Funding provides a project with cash that does not need to be repaid. Federal grants are considered funding. The federal government spends the money for the project to get built, with no expectation of being repaid.

Financing provides cash to build a project today, but that cash is borrowed and will need to be repaid with interest in the future. In the past, financing has primarily come from private investors who purchase bonds or invest directly in a project. More recently the federal government has also offered financing programs as well as direct funding.

Funding for large infrastructure projects is typically not available to cover the full cost of the project at its start. State and local agencies use financing to get the upfront cash needed for the project. The investors who provide the financing expect to be repaid, with interest, over time. Repayment can come from federal or state tax revenues, but it can also come from future user fees, dedicated sales taxes, new tax revenues that result from the project (e.g., increased economic activity from development), or other sources (such as revenues from concessions at rest stops or airports).

Both funding and financing play a critical role in getting infrastructure projects done. Financing allows projects to be completed faster—sometimes years faster than they could otherwise be done—and helps to spread the payments for an infrastructure asset over the life of the asset. Funding—from taxes, fees, or other revenue sources—is needed to repay financing.

Q: What is "innovative financing"?

A: In the infrastructure context, innovative financing typically refers to any type of financing other than standard tax-exempt municipal bonds. Tax-exempt bonds are issued by states, cities, counties, and other regional and local governmental or quasi-governmental entities to finance a range of public purposes, including infrastructure. Interest on these bonds is exempt from federal taxes, and therefore buyers of the bonds will accept a lower interest rate than they would for taxable bonds, since part of the income they receive on taxable bonds would have to be paid to the federal government. This reduces the cost of capital for local governments by lowering the interest rate that states and local governments have to pay to investors.

Tax-exempt debt is the primary way to finance infrastructure projects. Since the vast majority of buyers of tax-exempt debt are private companies and individuals, tax-exempt debt is one way to bring private investment into infrastructure.

In recent years, new financing options have emerged, including federally-supported programs such as the Transportation Infrastructure Finance and Innovation Act (TIFIA), which offers low-interest loans and loan guarantees for transportation projects; and private activity bonds, which allow certain types of public-private partnerships to issue tax-exempt debt, giving more types of projects access to bonds with the same preferential tax treatment as municipal bonds.

Some public-private partnerships use private sources of financing for projects. There are also emerging ways to structure debt like value capture—future increases in property tax revenues are pledged as repayment for a bond. Collectively these tools are known as innovative financing.

Q: Why do we need innovative financing?

A: America's tax-exempt bond market is the envy of the world. It has financed trillions of dollars in infrastructure projects. There are reasons why a community might pursue other financing methods.

- Some places are concerned that taking on more debt could adversely affect their credit rating, which could make future debt issuances more expensive for them.
- There may be public or political opposition to taking on more debt, or a strict schedule for debt issuances that would delay the project by months or even years.
- A few states and localities are at or near statutory debt limits.
- Using other forms of financing can free up capital raised

from prior debt issuances for other purposes.

- Innovative financing also draws capital from different types of investors; because of their tax-exempt status, municipal bonds do not attract investors who do not pay federal taxes anyway, such as pension funds, university endowments, and foreign investors.

Q: Are public-private partnerships a form of financing?

A: Sometimes. A public-private partnership can be a form of innovative financing, but it does not have to be. Many of these contractual arrangements involve private financing, but some do not.

In a typical infrastructure project, a public agency contracts with separate private companies to complete each stage of the project: design and engineering; construction; and sometimes operations and maintenance.

In a P3, a public agency contracts with a single private partner (typically a consortium of companies) to complete multiple stages of the project. Putting responsibility for multiple project stages into the hands of a single consortium can save time, encourage best practices (since the same consortium will build what they design, or operate what they build), and protect the public agency from risks, such as cost increases or schedule delays.

As part of the contract, many P3s require the private partner to provide the upfront capital for the project, to be paid back over time from project revenues or payments from the public partner. When this is the case, P3s can be considered a form of financing. In very few cases do P3s actually provide private funding for a project.

Q: What does it mean to say we can leverage private dollars with public funds?

A: This use of leverage is different from the technical financial meaning—the ratio of debt to equity in a project or investment. In the infrastructure context, leveraging private dollars means that an investment of public funds into a project is expected to attract private dollars to that project as well. This can happen in several ways.

For example, a public agency may be working with a private consortium to develop a project, and neither the public agency nor the private partner has the ability to finance the entire project on its own. In that case, a low-interest loan from the federal TIFIA program might be able to fill the gap, allowing the project to move forward with private financing covering the rest. It might be said that the TIFIA loan leveraged the private capital for the project.

Tax credits for private investments in infrastructure are another way to use public funds to leverage private dollars. Under this type of structure, a private company will invest dollars directly in an infrastructure project, and will receive a credit on its federal taxes equal to a specified percentage of that investment. The public investment is the revenue loss from the tax credit, but by providing an incentive for private investment, tax credits are expected to leverage a greater amount of private investment than they cost the federal government.

Q: Do funding and financing have different impacts on the federal budget?

A: Funding and financing are scored differently for federal budget purposes. Grant programs score at their full dollar amount, although the costs may be spread over several years. For example, a $100 million grant program would ultimately cost the federal government $100 million.

Federal financing programs are scored differently. In the case of a loan program, the cost to the federal government is the amount of the loan multiplied by the risk that the loan will not be paid back. So a $100 million loan with a 10 percent default risk would score for federal budget purposes at $10 million. For federal budget purposes, a program that provides infrastructure loans would have a smaller budgetary impact than a similarly sized grant program. However, from the state and local perspective, federal loans are more costly than federal grants, as loans require interest payments and grants do not.

Q: Is a national infrastructure bank funding or financing?

A: A national infrastructure bank could provide either funding or financing, or both, depending on what Congress authorized. Congress could create a bank with the authority to provide grants (which would be funding) or loans and loan guarantees (which would be financing). Authorizing a bank to allocate private activity bonds among projects, something USDOT now does for transportation projects, would also be a form of financing support.

Q: Were (proposed) repatriated corporate profits used to pay for infrastructure, as some have suggested, would it be funding or financing?

A: It depends on how Congress decides to use them. If those dollars were to be used to pay for grants, that is a source of funding. If they are used to support lending programs, that would be a source of financing.

https://bipartisanpolicy.org/blog/
infrastructure-finance-faqs/

A Guide to Infrastructure Bonds
Bipartisan Policy Center, Jan. 24, 2017
By Sarah Kline, Fellow

For years, the municipal bond market has been the primary source of capital for U.S. infrastructure. Recently, other types of bonds have also played a role in financing projects. This post compares three types of bonds that are or have been used for infrastructure: tax-exempt bonds, direct payment bonds, and private activity bonds.

These bonds are a form of debt issued by state or local governments, and all are subsidized by the federal government. The bonds differ from each other in two key ways: (1) what projects are eligible, and (2) what type of federal support they receive.

—

Tax-Exempt Bonds

Tax-exempt bonds, also known as municipal bonds or "muni" bonds, are issued by state and local governments and other governmental entities to raise capital for public purposes. Because investors don't pay federal taxes on the interest they earn, they are willing to accept a lower interest rate than they would on a taxable bond, making financing cheaper for state and local governments. The federal government incurs a cost from these bonds in terms of foregone tax revenue.

Advantages:
- These bonds can be used for all types of publicly owned infrastructure.
- The tax-exempt bond market is very deep and liquid, with millions of investors.
- Transactions are standardized and information about issuers' creditworthiness is readily available, keeping transaction costs low.

Limitations:
- Tax-exempt bonds are generally only available for projects that are publicly owned and managed, which

prevents many public-private partnerships from qualifying and limits localities' ability to transfer projects
built with tax-exempt financing to private ownership or
management.

- The tax exemption makes these bonds attractive to
investors with federal tax liability but not to investors
who do not pay federal taxes, such as pension funds, life
insurance companies, and funds run by foreign governments (known as "sovereign wealth funds").

Given America's broad needs and the wide range of potential investors, financing options should include all of the above.

—

Direct Payment Bonds

Direct payment bonds are another form of state and local
government debt. Unlike tax-exempt bonds, the interest on
direct payment bonds is taxable. Because purchasers of these
bonds will have to pay taxes on the interest, they require a higher
interest rate than they would on tax-exempt bonds. Rather than
using a tax exemption to make this form of financing cheaper
for state and local governments, the federal government makes a
direct payment to the state or local issuer of the bond, equal to a
specified percentage of the interest. In effect, the federal government pays a portion of the interest on the bond.

This type of bond was authorized for a limited period in
the 2009 American Recovery and Reinvestment Act under the
name "Build America Bonds," or "BABs." Over the next two
years, $181 billion in BABs were issued. Under the BABs pro-
gram, the federal government provided a payment to state and
local issuers equal to 35 percent of interest. The Obama administration's proposal to reauthorize BABs would have lowered
the payment to 28 percent of interest—reducing the cost to the
federal government but also reducing the benefit to state and
local governments.

Advantages:

- Direct payment bonds are attractive to both investors that do not pay federal taxes and to investors that do. They are attractive to investors that do not pay federal taxes because the value of the bond does not depend on the purchaser's tax status (unlike tax-exempt bonds, where part of the value comes from the tax exemption). Investors who do pay federal taxes will still purchase these bonds because the higher interest rate compensates for the federal tax liability.
- Federal payments go directly to state and local governments rather than to investors through a tax exemption. Economic studies have shown that investors in tax-exempt bonds absorb some of that benefit rather than passing its full value along to state and local issuers in the form of lower interest rates.

Limitations:

- New bond programs can take time to get up and running. State and local governments had to pay relatively high fees to securities firms to develop required documents and market BABs to potential buyers at the beginning of the program (though these fees had dropped by the time the program ended).
- Like tax-exempt bonds, BABs were available only for publicly-owned projects.
- The BABs program was authorized for two years, so only projects and investors who were "ready to go" could utilize the program. (This issue is not inherent to direct payment bonds, and a future authorization could be for a longer period.)
- The direct payment to issuers was reduced by the 2013 sequester, undermining confidence in the program.

—

Private Activity Bonds

Private activity bonds, or "PABs," support the development

of projects that are owned or managed by a private entity. Like municipal bonds, PABs offer tax-exempt interest as long as the bond is issued to finance a qualifying project. The types of projects that qualify under current law include airports, docks, and water and sewer facilities, among others.

Advantages:

- PABs bring the benefits of tax-exempt debt to privately owned or managed projects that have a public purpose.
- Like tax-exempt debt, PABs are issued by a public agency, but payment of principal and interest comes from the private partner and don't impact the public agency's credit rating or debt limit.

Limitations:

- Like muni debt, PABs are less attractive to investors who do not have federal tax liability.
- While interest on PABs is generally exempted from federal income taxes, it is subject to the Alternative Minimum Tax (AMT), so purchasers of these bonds will require higher interest than traditional tax-exempt debt, making this form of financing more costly.
- PABs currently have a statutory "volume cap" that limits the amount that may be issued in each state. Transportation-related PABs have a separate authorization totaling $15 billion, which is allocated among qualifying projects by the Department of Transportation.

—

Move America Bonds

A note about recently proposed Move America bonds, a specific type of private activity bond: Like other PABs, Move America bonds could be issued by public entities on behalf of a private partner for a qualifying infrastructure project. Move America bonds would have their own volume cap, separate from other PABs. Unlike traditional PABs, Move America bonds would not be subject to the AMT, making them more attractive to investors who are subject to that tax and keeping interest rates more in line with traditional tax-exempt debt. Move America Bonds could also be converted into tax credits, a topic that will be covered in a separate post.

—

The Bipartisan Policy Council Executive Council on Infrastructure, in its 2016 report, recommended that the well-established tax-exempt bond market, which has proven to be an extremely effective way to support infrastructure, be preserved; that private activity bonds be expanded to ensure that public-private partnerships can access tax-preferred financing; and that taxable direct payment bonds should be made available again to attract a broader range of investors.

These goals could also be accomplished through a combined approach: complementing the existing tax-exempt market with a new direct payment bond for which all projects with a public purpose, whether publicly or privately owned, are eligible.

https://bipartisanpolicy.org/blog/a-guide-to-infrastructure-bonds/

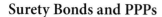

Surety Bonds and PPPs

The National Association of Surety Bond Producers (NASBP.org) describes a surety bond as "a promise to be liable for the debt, default, or failure of another. It is a three-party contract by which one party (the surety) guarantees the performance or obligations of a second party (the principal) to a third party (the obligee)."

Surety bonds are sold by insurance companies and range from the mundane—a bail bond in the case of an arrest is a surety bond—to complex, high-stakes financial transactions where failure would be catastrophic, as it was in the case of the fraud and collapse of Enron Energy in 2001.

Surety coverage is so reliable that even when the company's insurers tried to get off the hook by proving they had been duped, they still ended up having to pay out nearly $1 billion to Enron's victims because, as the New York Times *noted, "In the surety bond field, coverage is generally extended only after careful study of financial statements and other signs of business health." In the case of Enron, the surety companies didn't do their homework.*

In the case of infrastructure joint ventures, contract surety bonds are standard operating procedure and, as noted in Chapter 6, have often protected the public when PPP contractors ran into financial trouble. When a public entity (the obligee) partners with a contractor (the principal) to build a highway or provide a public service, the contractor must obtain a surety bond that guarantees if the contractor defaults, the surety company will find another contractor to complete the contract without any cost to taxpayers. The following information is excerpted from the NASBP website.

There are four types of contract surety bonds:

- Bid Bond: Provides financial protection to the owner if a bidder is awarded a contract but fails to sign the contract or provide the required performance and payment bonds.
- Performance Bond: Provides an owner with a guarantee that, in the event of a contractor's default, the surety will complete or cause to be completed the contract.
- Payment Bond: Ensures that certain subcontractors and suppliers will be paid for labor and materials incorporated into a construction contract.
- Warranty Bond (also called a Maintenance Bond): Guarantees the owner that any workmanship and material defects found in the original construction will be repaired during the warranty period.

—

When Do I Need A Contract Surety Bond?

Any federal construction contract valued at $150,000 or more requires surety bonds when a contractor bids or as a condition of contract award. Most state and municipal governments have a similar requirement.

—

What Are Surety Companies?

Most surety bonds in the US are written by subsidiaries or divisions of insurance companies. Surety companies typically are authorized and qualified to do business by the state insurance commissioner where they are domiciled and in the jurisdiction where the bond is issued.

—

Surety bonds … are risk transfer mechanisms. Traditional insurance is a two-party agreement designed to compensate the insured against unforeseen adverse events. Surety companies operate on a different business model. Surety bonds are three-party agreements designed to prevent a loss. The surety does not assume the primary obligation but is secondarily liable if the principal defaults on its bonded obligation.

The surety underwriting is a form of credit, much like a lending arrangement. For contract surety, for instance, the surety will examine in-depth the contractor's credit history and financial strength, experience, equipment, work in progress, management capacity, and character. After the surety assesses such factors, it makes a determination as to the appropriateness and the amount, if any, of surety credit and the cost of coverage.

If the surety extends surety credit to a contractor, the surety … expects the bonded contractor to perform its obligations successfully (under a) general agreement of indemnity, or GIA … a powerful legal document. … A surety company almost always requires that the principal, the individuals who own and/or control the company, their spouses, and often affiliated companies to sign the GIA before it will issue bonds on behalf of the contractor.

—

Who Are Surety Bond Producers?

Obtaining surety credit starts with professional bond producers. Arranging bonds and a line of credit with a surety company requires extensive, detailed work for every bid. Each surety company has its own unique underwriting standards and practices, and the pre-qualification process to obtain surety credit can be a difficult experience if not handled by a surety bond specialist.

Bond producers must be licensed by the state(s) in which they do business. … Unlike most insurance agents, surety bond producers focus their main activities on the surety market and positioning construction firms to qualify for surety credit.

A bond producer can serve as an objective, external resource for evaluating a construction firm's capabilities and can suggest improvements to help the construction firm meet a surety company's underwriting requirements.

A long-term, successful relationship between the producer

and the contractor can be beneficial for the growth and development of the construction firm. In choosing a bond producer, construction firms should consider the following in the selection process.

- Is the producer licensed in your jurisdiction and that of the project?
- Does the producer have a reputation for integrity?
- What percentage of business are construction clients?
- Do they understand the construction industry and the construction process, particularly the management and administration of construction contracts?
- Do they understand construction accounting procedures, especially an ability to analyze financial statements, work in progress, and cash flow?
- With how many sureties does the producer work?
- Is the producer authorized to issue bonds on behalf of sureties?
- Has the producer developed solid relationships with surety underwriters?
- Has the producer developed solid relationships with other professional service providers, such as CPAs, attorneys, and lenders?
- How aware of and interested is the producer in local, regional, and national construction markets?
- How active is the producer in local or national construction associations and in local or national surety industry associations?
- Is the producer committed to frequent client contact through newsletters, site visits, and visits to client offices?

What Do Surety Bonds Cost?

Like life insurance, surety bonds are an expense. Surety-Info.org is a robust website with a great deal of detailed information. Here is some excerpted material:

Surety bond premiums vary from one surety to another, but can range from 0.5% to 3% of the contract amount, depending on the size, type, and duration of the project and the contractor. Typically, there is no direct charge for a bid bond, and in many cases, performance bonds incorporate payment bonds and maintenance bonds.

When bonds are specified in the contract, it is the contractor's responsibility to obtain the bonds. The contractor generally includes the bond premium amount in the bid, and the premium generally is payable upon execution of the bond.

If the contract amount changes, the premium will be adjusted for the change. Payment and performance bonds typically are priced based on the value of the contract being bonded, not necessarily on the size of the bond.

The US Small Business Administration (SBA) has a Surety Bond Guarantee (SBG) program that helps small and emerging contractors obtain bonds. Contact the SBA Office of Surety Bond Guarantees at www.sba.gov/surety-bonds. Suretylearn. org has additional resources about how small and emerging contractors can obtain surety credit.

The Surety & Fidelity Association of America (SFAA) has current surety industry information at www.surety.org. Free publications are available from the Surety Information Office (SIO) at www.sio.org, including "The Importance of Surety Bonds in Construction n Helping Contractors Grow," "Surety Bonding for New & Emerging Contractors," "Surety Companies: What They Are & How to Find Out About Them," and "The Importance of Surety Bonds in Construction."

—

Other sources of information about surety companies can be found at each state's insurance department which is responsible for licensing and is responsible for periodic examinations of the company and its financial health. Insurance departments are located in the state capital and, in some instances, have offices in larger cities.

The US Treasury Department maintains a list of surety companies that it has deemed qualified to write surety bonds required by the federal government and develops a dollar underwriting limitation for each company. This list is published annually and updated throughout the year. The most current list of Treasury-authorized companies is available at:

https://www.fiscal.treasury.gov/fsreports/ref/suretyBnd/c570.htm.

—

A.M. Best Company is a private publishing company that analyzes and rates insurance companies. Each year it publishes a detailed profile and financial information on almost all insurance companies operating in the US, giving each an alphabetic rating and a financial size category. The book can be found in many public and financial libraries.

—

Insurance Agents and Brokers

Most surety bonds are issued through insurance agents and brokers who can provide information regarding a specific company.

A Glossary of Common Surety Bond Terms:
https://www.suretybonds.com/glossary.html

Surety Bonds Versus Letters of Credit:
Trends in PPP Contracts
By James Bly, National At-Large Director
Construction Financial Management Association
Construction Executive Magazine, Nov, 9, 2016

Some US sureties are providing pay-on-demand bond forms that read like an irrevocable letter of credit (LOC) for owners that do not recognize the value of the accelerated adjudication process in (surety) bond forms.

—

Because subcontractors and suppliers are unable to perfect a lien on P3 projects, surety bonds that include a performance bond with an accelerated dispute resolution process or liquidity feature, as well as a payment bond for the protection of the subcontractors and suppliers, remains the security of choice for the benefit of all project participants.

If LOCs are used in lieu of surety bonds, subcontractors and suppliers will have no recourse against the bank that issues the letter of credit, leaving them exposed to the contractor's default risk.

Two of the top three sureties have been leaders in the P3 market, developing performance bonds that include an accelerated dispute resolution process that meets the liquidity needs of the concessionaire and its lender, while providing payment bonds that give protection to subcontractors and suppliers.

One surety has developed a hybrid performance bond that includes a pay-on-demand feature for a percentage of the bond penalty with the balance of the bond coming under the accelerated adjudication process. The accelerated adjudication process guarantees a decision to the obligee within a short period of time through the use of alternate dispute resolution processes.

Conditional surety bonds used on P3 projects also benefit the design-build contractor. The built-in adjudication process included in the bond form reduces the contractor's exposure to a liquidity crisis. When an irrevocable letter of credit is called, the bank must immediately pay, and the amount paid promptly converts to bank debt. Contractors and their banks are not given an opportunity to dispute the reasons for the default, and the contractor's liquidity is impacted even when the contractor has a legitimate defense to the claim. With a surety bond, the surety must weigh the merits of a surety bond default versus the contractor's defenses.

The surety has to follow legal duties, including timely response to the demand, evaluation of the contractor's defenses to the default and responding in good faith to the claimant. The surety must respond under the terms of a bond for all valid claims, including paying for damages up to the penalty of the bond, financing the defaulted contractor to completion or hiring a replacement contractor.

The surety cannot force the contractor to perform if the contractor has valid defenses to the default. The surety claim process has the advantage of preserving the contractor's liquidity throughout the course of a dispute on a bonded contract until the facts are reviewed and a bond coverage determination is reached.

—

Some owners or lenders will avoid conditional payment surety bonds at all cost and demand letters of credit. A few sureties are looking to provide bank syndication guarantees where the sureties become a participant on bank letters of credit guaranteeing up to 50 percent of the irrevocable LOC in a reinsurance agreement with the bank.

Sureties also are becoming more sophisticated creditors through inter-creditor agreements that clearly define the first and second security positions for the banks and bonding companies, helping the surety expand capacity with these new products.

http://enewsletters.construction-exec.com/managingyourbusiness/2016/11/suretys-impact-on-emerging-trends-in-public-construction/

PPPs Hedge Managed Toll Lane Risks
by Robert Poole, Director of Transportation Policy
Reason Foundation, May 6, 2015

Reason Foundation is a libertarian think tank which publishes a great deal of useful, timely material on its website, Reason.Org, and is available to the general public as part of its mission. The following excerpts are included to provide some insights into the financial details of tollway projects.

The P3 community has been eagerly awaiting Virginia's third express toll lanes project—I-66 outside the Beltway. Estimated to cost between $2 billion and $3 billion, the project would convert the existing HOV (high occupancy vehicle) lane and add a new express toll lane each way, for a distance of 25 miles. Three or four teams were being assembled, and expectations were high that the process would begin soon.

Now there are rumblings of concern over whether the Virginia Department of Transportation (VDOT) actually intends to offer the I-66 project as a toll concession. VDOT Secretary Aubrey Layne (see Chapter 8 for other details) said, "We generally thought that [I-66] would lend itself to a P3 … we believe there are available funds we can raise to do that through other federal programs." Compared with previous P3 projects, "… the board has monies, and initiating tolling is not the risk that it was in previous deals."

Ed Regan, Senior Vice President of CDM Smith (a Philadelphia-based infrastructure engineering and construction firm) … points out that compared with revenue projections on conventional toll road projects, the revenue on a managed lane is very sensitive to small changes in demand. For example, a 10% increase in corridor traffic might mean a 30% increase in revenue, but this cuts both ways—a 10% traffic decrease in corridor traffic due to a recession could mean 30% less revenue. In addition, revenue in the early years of a managed lane is typically low. Compared with traditional toll roads, managed lanes revenue is somewhat less predictable and less stable, especially in the early years. Longer term, the revenue growth is likely to be greater.

Rating agencies consider managed lanes a good fit for P3 concessions, because compared with typical public sector all-debt financing, the equity investment in a concession provides a cushion during the early years. If toll revenue is below forecast in a $1 billion 100% debt-financed project, debt service must still be paid on the $1 billion. But if 25% of the $1 billion was equity (generating revenue), debt service payments can still be made, even if initial toll revenue is well below forecast.

Fitch Ratings and Standard & Poor's each released reports on managed lane projects in 2012, in both cases focusing on P3 projects in which the new capacity is paid for via toll-based finance. Fitch states that "It is [our] expectation that managed lane revenue will behave like a derivative, meaning as general purpose lane volume grows, managed lane revenue will grow at faster rates.

"When the amount of general purpose traffic declines, managed lane traffic and revenue will drop more." Fitch went on to say, "Given this volatility, higher liquidity levels throughout the life of the debt are critical to help support cash flow during periods of economic weakness. All else being equal, a managed lane project rated 'BBB' needs to have more financial flexibility ... than a typical toll road given the potential volatility in annual cash flow."

S&P points out that even a mature project like the Interstate 91 Express Lanes in California has suffered toll revenue declines during recessions.

As Virginia DOT (and other state DOTs) consider whether to do a managed lanes mega-project in-house or via a P3 toll concession, it's easy to imagine public officials with visions of surplus toll revenues in the later years of the project asking themselves why they should let a private sector company have all that revenue in the out-years. There certainly is long-term potential for such revenues, but deciding whether it's in the public interest to do the project as a P3 concession must balance possible future revenues against the possibility of early-year losses due to volatility of traffic and revenue.

A good example is the Interstate 495 Express Lanes on the Washington, DC Beltway in northern Virginia. The first two years of traffic and revenue were below projections, so the concession company restructured the project's finances, increasing its equity investment by 80%. Had VDOT done the project, would it have been prepared to invest an additional $280 million in its second year? That kind of traffic and revenue risk transfer is part of the value proposition for doing this kind of project as a P3 toll concession.

As for the potential surplus revenue in the out-years, the answer is to build into the concession agreement a predefined revenue-sharing provision with the state DOT. That's especially appropriate if the state DOT makes an initial investment in the project, as VDOT did on the Beltway project (whose concession agreement does include revenue sharing).

http://reason.org/news/show-how-risky-are-managed-lane-concessi

PPP Case Studies

Case Studies: An Overview
Bipartisan Policy Center
[Excerpted]

A review of select US public-private partnership projects yields four important lessons for any state and local governments that are broadly applicable and serve as a baseline for understanding the role of P3s in addressing the nation's infrastructure challenges.

1. The private sector can play different roles depending on the needs of the project.

P3s can be used as a tool for increased expectation of on-time delivery and reduced risk for the public agency. For a large project that costs more than a state or locality can provide with conventional financing, a private partner can help bridge the gap. The Dulles Greenway (a toll road in Northern Virginia) was largely financed by a private partner. The Commonwealth of Virginia paid the higher cost for private financing rather than taking on a large public debt issuance. Without private financing, the Greenway would likely not have been built.

In some cases, the private partner serves both needs— project delivery and financing. In the case of the Port Miami Tunnel, the private partner took on the difficult task of delivering a tunnel in an urban area, bearing the risk of construction delays and providing upfront financing. The Florida Department of Transportation will repay the costs over time.

2. There is no one-size-fits-all.

While many P3s involve toll facilities (tolls are a clear source of revenue to pay back private financing costs), newer structures have emerged. The city of Miami elected to not implement tolls on its new tunnel to avoid dissuading drivers from using it. Instead, the private partners will be paid over time with milestone and availability payments from state and local revenues.

There is a misperception that P3s can only be used for mega-projects. The city of Detroit opted for a P3 for its Metro Freeway Lighting project to increase safety, visibility, and energy efficiency. The Pennsylvania Rapid Bridge Replacement project (see Chapter XX) bundled more than 550 small bridge projects into a single procurement to take advantage of the economies of scale that a P3 could offer. This model can potentially be used elsewhere to complete multiple smaller projects that states do not have the capacity to address all at once.

3. The benefits of private involvement in infrastructure are often overlooked.

While the cost of private capital is well understood and it is easy to calculate the total costs of construction and financing, it is more difficult to put a dollar figure on the benefits of long-term asset maintenance and the transfer of risks. As a result, the benefits of P3s are often undervalued, especially that risks can be shared between the public and private partners.

In the case of the (Virginia) Dulles Greenway and the Indiana Toll Road, most of the demand risk (i.e., the risk that the toll road would not be used as much as projected) was transferred from the public sector to the private sector. As a result, the public would not be on the hook for the costs of maintaining the roadways should toll revenues be insufficient. This protection against future liabilities has economic value but is rarely quantified.

There is also a significant benefit to the public sector of locking in long-term operations and maintenance costs. When appropriate protections are included in the contract for quality control, the public can guarantee a well-maintained asset without having to absorb unexpected future costs or compete for adequate funding in the legislature. The Pennsylvania Rapid Bridge Replacement project, for example, locks in maintenance costs for the next 25 years.

4. Few projects are a 100 percent success or a 100 percent failure.

P3s are complex transactions with multiple parties. Evaluating them requires an understanding of how the needs of multiple stakeholders are being addressed. For example, the Indiana Toll Road is sometimes referred to as a "failed" P3. However, it is only a failure from the perspective of the original private consortium, which declared bankruptcy after toll revenues did not meet projections amid the economic recession. (See Chapter 15)

From the state's perspective, however, the people of Indiana received a benefit in the form of the original upfront payment from the private consortium, as well as the existence of the toll road itself.

The P3 structure is continually evolving to fit the needs of communities of many sizes and varieties.

https://bipartisanpolicy.org/infrastructure-case-studies/

Case Study: P3 Financial Analysis

One of the first questions asked by those who are just learning about public-private partnerships is, "Where is the money coming from to finance this project?"

The short answer is that it comes from investors—typically institutions like pension funds, insurance companies, and conservative, income-oriented money managers. Pension plans in particular are looking for "high-quality, long-duration fixed income securities like private debt to help match liabilities instead of simply using government debt," according to Carlo DiLalla, vice president and chief portfolio manager for fixed income at CIBC Asset Management.

In September, 2017, DiLalla told Canada's *Financial Post* that CIBC is launching a new fund with plans to invest up to $700 million annually in 10 to 15 projects, "the bulk of which will be in private P3's, investments with terms of 25 to 30 years." DiLalla said the yield on P3 private debt is expected to be between 4 and 4.5 percent, higher than the yield on similar publicly traded investments.

One of the big attractions is that investors in P3 private debt are exposed to less risk and volatility than in publicly-traded debt. P3 bonds turned out to be been a safe haven in the turbulence that followed the credit crisis in 2008. By 2011, longer-dated P3 bonds had outperformed all other bonds in Canada. Smart investors began to sit up and take notice that P3s are not that sensitive to economic ups and downs because private investors are more disciplined and demanding in managing risk.

The proposed sale of P3 private debt is subject to layers of risk analysis and assigned a credit rating. For example, the following is from a credit report prepared by Standard & Poor's (S&P) of the proposed infrastructure joint venture that bundled the repair and 25-year maintenance contract for more than 550 Pennsylvania bridges. (See Chapter 12). It is included here to show what investors look at when considering the financial rationale for a P3. The full report can be found on the website of the Association for the Improvement of American Infrastructure (aiai-infra.info).

—

From Standard & Poor's Ratings Services
Project & Infrastructure Ratings Team
"Plenary Walsh Keystone Partners LLC (PWKP)
Assigned Preliminary 'BBB' Rating: Outlook Stable"
Feb 5, 2015

Overview Of The Project
- Under a concession agreement with the Pennsylvania Department of Transportation (PennDOT), PWKP will develop, design, construct and maintain 558 bridges throughout the state.
- We have assigned our preliminary 'BBB' rating; stable outlook.
- The Pennsylvania Economic Development Financing Authority (PEDFA) will issue $732 million in tax-exempt private activity revenue bonds (PABs) which will be on-lent to the project. Estimated costs are $900 million and the project receives $225M in milestone payments.
- Overall construction period is estimated at 36 months (end of 2017) and operating and maintenance (O&M) phase is 25 years from substantial project completion.
- There is no volume risk. The project will receive monthly availability payments that will be used to service debt and to maintain the bridges.

The project's total construction cost is estimated at about $900 million. During the 36-month construction phase, the project will receive \$224.75 million in milestone and mobilization payments from PennDOT.

The "BBB" rating reflects our view of the following strengths:

- The project has a strong counter-party in PennDOT, which will make progress and availability payments to the project during construction and operations, respectively.
- The project has a well-developed concession agreement with clear and logical risk allocation with terms consistent with those of similar P3 projects we have rated.
- The project has an experienced design-and-build joint venture. Also, most of the construction will be done by local subcontractors that have worked in the region and are PennDOT approved. We view the the joint venture as having sufficient project management experience for a project of this type, which principally presents logistical and schedule management risks.
- The construction plan is straightforward, with very limited geotechnical risk. Although the number of bridges to be replaced is high at 558, they are simple structures and on average span about 50 feet.
- In the event of a contractor default or inability to complete the project, we consider the (joint venture) replaceable, and the security package robust enough to not tie the project rating to the credit quality of the joint venture participants during the construction phase. Based on the liquidity package, we view project liquidity as adequate to replace the major contractor and minor subcontractor. The liquidity for the replacement scenario will represent about 6% of the construction price and comes from a combination of letters of credit (LOCs) from the joint venture, a retention account, and performance bond proceeds.
- During the operating phase, liquidity is in line with that

of comparable P3 peers and consists of a six months' debt service reserve and a three-year look-forward major maintenance reserve.

- Given that this is an availability project with low maintenance requirements, we anticipate unusually stable cash flows during the operating phase. Our base case includes a 5% increase in operating, maintenance, and lifecycle costs over management's case, and inflation assumed to be 2% per annum. The project has demonstrated cash flow resiliency under our downside case, which includes an additional 10% stress over our base case.

Partly offsetting the above strengths, in our view, are the following weaknesses:

- Although construction is fairly simple and straightforward, traffic management and acquiring right of way are of concern in meeting the construction schedule. However, the construction schedule has sufficient slack to accommodate any delays.
- The project will contract out maintenance to (a vendor) which is experienced in managing infrastructure projects but has limited experience in managing such a unique project. To reflect this concern, we increased by 5% our base case assumed maintenance costs. Unanticipated cost increases above this level could weaken debt service coverage.
- The project is exposed to inflation, in that 90% of availability payments received from PennDOT are fixed and the remaining 10% are indexed to the consumer price index.

—

http://aiai-infra.info/members-only/wp-content/uploads/2015/02/Plenary-Walsh-Keystone-Partners-PRESALE-REPORT.pdf

Case Study: Colorado Community Engagement
Boulder High Performance Transportation Enterprise
Association for the Improvement of American Infrastructure

The state of Colorado is among the nation's most successful adopters of high-profile civic and transportation P3 projects. Since 2007, various groups have teamed with private partners to initiate multiple P3 projects including the US 36 Express Lanes Project, the Regional Transportation District's FasTracks mass transit program and Denver's Union Station redevelopment. State and local agencies are also working together and planning to use the P3 approach to begin redevelopment of the National Western Center, a Colorado landmark and heritage site.

The positive experiences have resulted in fast-track project deliveries, local and regional economic development, and continued successful operations. Political, agency and private sector leaders believe the success of these projects is directly attributed to their focused emphasis on community outreach programs that have evolved since the early days of P3 initiation a decade ago. The following story spotlights some of the community engagement best practices that continue to enable the success of the region's P3 project delivery.

Corridor Connections

The US 36 Express Lanes Project was completed in 2016 [and] links the city of Boulder at the University of Colorado, Boulder's main campus, to downtown Denver. It incorporates a new express lane for bus rapid transit, carpool vehicles, and tolled vehicles, as well as two free general purpose lanes in each direction, a bikeway and the reconstruction of aging bridges.

The delivery of the project was split into two phases: a $318 million first phase procured as a design-build contract, and a $179 million second phase procured as a P3, with the concessionaire to finance, design and build phase two and operate and maintain the entire system once built out.

The complex project required coordination with a number

of cities along the route. Funding was multi-sourced with some Transportation Infrastructure Finance and Innovation Act (TIFIA) financing, as well as anticipated toll revenue.

The project began with a National Environmental Policy Act and Environmental Impact Statement process, both of which required intense and lengthy participation from local governments and the public. HPTE Director David Spector recalls, "We followed the NEPA rules regarding public involvement, engagement and education. We engaged all of the stakeholder communities up and down the corridor, which included multiple municipalities, counties, towns and cities. We provided annual reports to our state legislature. We did exactly what we were supposed to do based on all of our experiences with other project delivery methods, and quickly found out that it wasn't enough."

CDOT and HPTE faced many questions and some backlash from the community and public figures. The state legislature developed and passed a bill that would have required, among other things, greater transparency measures on P3 projects. The bill was vetoed but the governor issued an executive order which mandated appropriate transparency measures.

Spector says, "We failed to provide enough education about how a P3 project works, and who pays. Since then, we've introduced public outreach programs that are far more extensive."

Standard community engagement methods now include posting online every stage of the process along with press releases, bilingual messaging, open outreach at community groups and telephone town halls: a group of subject matter experts sits in a room and calls all of the phone numbers in the affected area, connecting them to the town hall discussion. Individuals are able to listen in and ask questions. While the in-person town hall had about 100 in attendance, the telephone town hall reached over 2,200. Possible future forums might include Facebook Live.

AIAI-Infra.org

Case Study: Kentucky Broadband Service
First Fiber-Optic P3 in the US
By The Bipartisan Policy Center, 2015
[Excerpted]

Project:
A $343.5 million design-build-finance-operate-maintain agreement to provide expanded access to high speed internet across Kentucky, financed by state bonds, senior tax-exempt revenue bonds, and senior taxable revenue bonds. Revenue includes user (service) fees, commercialization of excess capacity, and $23.5 million in federal grants.

—

Overview:
"KentuckyWired" is a statewide broadband project to build the infrastructure for high-speed internet access. It has two main objectives: to significantly improve bandwidth speeds and service reliability to government sites throughout Kentucky; and to promote growth by making the network's excess capacity available to commercial users. This capacity commercialization will be on an open access basis, making it far easier for internet service providers (ISPs) to service customers in rural and remote areas of the commonwealth.

In 2015, Kentucky entered into a 30-year public-private partnership (P3) with Macquarie Capital along with five private sector partners to design, build, finance, operate and maintain the broadband network.

—

Project Description:
In 2012 and 2013, the Shaping Our Appalachian Region Broadband Working Group recommended that the state should invest in an expansive, high-speed fiber-optic infrastructure to promote connectivity across Kentucky's rural, urban, and suburban communities (in light of) a considerable increase in the number of individual budget requests for funding for

high-speed fiber network upgrades.

Following the recommendation, Kentucky's Finance and Administration Cabinet began a screening process to find the best way to improve internet access and speed across the commonwealth. It was determined that rather than fulfilling each request individually, the best approach would be a single initiative through a P3.

In 2015, this plan materialized as the KentuckyWired project, promising to connect all 120 counties by 2019. While the commonwealth will maintain ownership of the system, it will be fully implemented by the private sector over a 30-year contract term, overseen by Macquarie Capital as the lead developer.

To create the system, Macquarie established a consortium with Macquarie, Ledcor, and First Solutions as equity investors, respectively holding 75 percent, 15 percent, and 10 percent of the company. Ledcor and Black & Veatch are 50 percent partners in the design/build venture, supported by Fujitsu and Bowlin as key subcontractors. Ledcor and Fujitsu will also be responsible for the system's operations and maintenance.

Along with $30 million allocated from the state budget and $23.5 million in federal grants, the Kentucky Economic Development Finance Authority issued $232 million in senior tax-exempt revenue bonds, and $58 million in senior taxable revenue bonds on behalf of KentuckyWired. Kentucky's public technology authority, the Kentucky Communications Network Authority, will manage the contract on behalf of the commonwealth and oversee the private partner's delivery of the KentuckyWired network.

When completed, this network will include over 3,200 miles of fiber-optic cable across the state and connect directly to about 1,100 government facilities (including K-12 schools, community colleges, and public universities), which will result in dramatically faster internet speeds in both rural and urban communities.

Approximately 50 percent of the fiber strands installed by

KentuckyWired will be available for commercial use by large scale enterprises and ISPs. This direct access to capacity should allow ISPs to offer higher speeds to homes and businesses. Macquarie will lead formation of a network wholesaler to market this excess capacity and plan to share a substantial portion of revenues generated from that activity with the commonwealth.

To generate revenue, the existing service fees will move from the carriers that currently hold service contracts to KentuckyWired. Kentucky is supporting the project with $30 million of bond-financed equipment, and will pay the consortium a $23.5 million milestone payment upon completing construction, in addition to a series of availability payments that are based on the system's performance.

—

Benefits and Criticisms:

As the definition of infrastructure changes to keep up with technology, broadband has carved out an important role. Kentucky ranks 47th in the country in broadband speeds and capacity. During peak-usage periods, Kentucky has the nation's slowest connection speed; 34 percent of Kentucky's residents do not have access to suitable broadband services; and 16 percent have no access.

Recognizing these inadequacies and the shifting economic pressures from a decline in the coal industry, Kentucky's policymakers envisioned a service rate platform that will extend from 100 megabits per second to 100 gigabits per second with multiple tiers, far surpassing the Federal Communications Commission's recommended minimum.

KentuckyWired has partnered with a number of local providers to build portions of the network on behalf of the private consortium. Anecdotal evidence suggests ISPs are reducing market pricing by up to a third for enterprise users to prepare for the competitive impact of the system's open access provisions.

From a deal-structure standpoint, the 30-year partnership

has received praise as Bond Buyer's 2015 "Deal of the Year," reaching financial close within nine months while transferring the long-term operation and maintenance risks to the private partners.

It was developed to avoid additional budget appropriation requirements from the commonwealth. As part of Kentucky-Wired's contract, a minimum of 60 percent of the employees on the project will be from Kentucky. The consortium of private companies has also committed to hiring local companies and workers.

Concerns have risen around a portion of funds from the FCC's E-Rate program that was previously allocated directly to public schools. When the commonwealth awarded KentuckyWired the contract to connect directly to public schools, the move was challenged as a conflict of interest that would disqualify the project from $11 million in federal funds. It is unclear if the state will need to replace the $11 million or if a new bidding process will take place.

The governor confirmed his commitment to the KentuckyWired project in September 2016, noting in particular the system's ability to deliver economic benefits, "especially in the eastern part of the state," which has been most impacted by the downturn in the coal industry.

Criticism has also come from local telecom companies that are concerned the project would be duplicative of their own network expansions. Others argue that, given the state of Kentucky's network, an intervention in the form of a P3 was a necessity.

Takeaways:
The project is the first fiber-optic P3 in the US and a monumental overhaul of Kentucky's broadband networks. Given the expanding role of the internet, ensuring reliable high-speed access is critical to the commonwealth's continued economic competitiveness and growth. By essentially bundling

the commonwealth's network needs, KentuckyWired attracted significant private sector financing while upgrading the infrastructure in rural and urban communities.

Case Study: Atlanta Braves and SunTrust Park
By The Bipartisan Policy Center

The Atlanta Braves and Cobb County Government, Georgia, established a public-private partnership for construction of a new 42,000-seat stadium—SunTrust Park—and The Battery Atlanta, a 1.5-million-square-foot mixed-use entertainment destination including restaurants featuring local chefs, fashion retailers, a bowling alley, and a 4,000-seat music venue. The project (opened in 2017) used a design-build-finance-operate-maintenance P3.

The total budget for the project was $672 million, with $300 million funded by Cobb County and the Cumberland Community Improvement District. The partnership will continue through 2046, during which time the Braves will have exclusive rights to operate and manage the stadium.

The County and the Braves will make equal annual contributions to a capital maintenance fund for capital improvements and repairs for the stadium and parking areas. During the contract, the stadium will be owned by the Cobb-Marietta Coliseum and Exhibit Hall Authority, an agency created by the Georgia General Assembly in 1980.

At the end of the contract, the Atlanta Braves have an option to purchase the stadium. If the Braves elect not to purchase the stadium, Cobb County would assume full ownership.

Case Study: Port of Miami Tunnel
By The Bipartisan Policy Center

The Port of Miami Tunnel (POMT) is an example of a design-build-finance-operate-maintain P3 for transportation infrastructure. The Port of Miami is located on an island. Prior to the opening of the POMT, traffic entering and exiting the Port of Miami, particularly large trucks, were forced to use city surface streets, creating considerable traffic congestion.

The motivating issue in the construction of the POMT was to divert this commercial traffic away from city streets. The idea of the POMT was first proposed in the 1980s, but the financing could never be secured.

The POMT P3 project began in 2009 and was completed in 2014. The total cost of design and construction was approximately $600 million. The private sector partner arranged for a substantial proportion of the upfront capital for the design and construction phases and will be operating and maintaining the tunnel until 2044.

The private sector partner receives availability payments not to exceed $32.5 million per year over the term of the contract. No vehicle tolls are being charged for use of the tunnel. However, the Florida Department of Transportation collects container and passenger fees that provide the revenue stream to finance the availability payments.

The POMT opened in August 2014 and is an example of how private sector financing can be used to advance the construction of a transportation asset when public funding is not available.

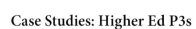

Case Studies: Higher Ed P3s

Using Public-Private Partnerships to
Create Higher Education Opportunities
By Stephen M. Jordan,
Charles A. Shorter, and Iris Weinshall
Trusteeship Magazine, January/February 2013
Association of Governing Boards
of Universities and Colleges

Overview:

Many independent colleges and universities have pursued partnerships with the private sector, but public institutions have largely shied away from them until now—as they are increasingly under pressure to find alternative sources of revenue.

In 2012, public institutions under pressure to find alternative sources of revenue to close gaps resulting from cutbacks in state appropriations accelerated development of P3s. *Trusteeship Magazine* asked leaders at institutions in two different cities to describe how public-private partnerships are helping further their goals.

—

Metropolitan State University of Denver

By Stephen M. Jordan, President

Metropolitan State University of Denver is Denver's newest hotelier. Our Hospitality Learning Center and adjacent Spring Hill Suites Denver Downtown opened last August on our campus. It's a major example of what we hope will be the first of many public-private partnerships that will benefit students' educational opportunities and our community long into the future.

When I was appointed in 2005, the board of trustees made it clear that it wanted to pursue a more entrepreneurial direction. There was a "sweet spot" for MSU Denver between two-year colleges that granted degrees focused primarily on workforce development and four-year research institutions—offering theory and practice for career-oriented students.

Our belief was that:

- Students should combine the analytic skills that come from the liberal arts with the work skills that students need to succeed.
- MSU Denver should turn out students that are workforce-ready.
- MSU Denver should collaborate with the community to identify essential areas of economic health that we can target with our academic programs.

When the economic downturn hit, such goals took on additional urgency and one more was added: find new sources of funding.

MSU Denver is relatively new, founded in 1965 to provide educational access and affordability to Coloradans in an urban environment. We are Colorado's most ethnically diverse four-year institution.

We share our campus with two other institutions—Community College of Denver and the University of Colorado Denver—in a unique partnership under the umbrella of the Auraria Higher Education Center (AHEC), our landowning entity.

Starting in 2005, MSU Denver leadership worked with AHEC to updated the 20 year-old campus master plan. Student growth at all three institutions was being accommodated willy-nilly; sometimes doublewide trailers had to be used for classrooms and office space.

Our representatives on the AHEC board of directors thought we needed to think about land use creatively. A public-private component was included in the request for proposals (RFP) that resulted in hiring campus planners and getting the process started.

The campus's prime location adjacent to a growing downtown created additional pressures; developers were eyeing our land as a possibility for a large retail store. During the two-year master planning process we made a commitment to not undertake any partnership because, in the words of one trustee, "We were not interested in having anyone on campus that doesn't have an integrated reason for being there."

Not long after that the hotel idea was hatched. The board assessed where higher education funding in Colorado was headed and ultimately determined that it would continue to diminish. At a board retreat, trustees decided that we should work toward creating partnerships that would produce revenue streams; support academic programs and student services, including more scholarships; and help connect MSU Denver more closely with the community.

A hotel was a natural fit. Our Department of Hospitality, Tourism and Events (HTE) has existed for 35 years and in the past six years the number of student majors doubled to 650. What we didn't have was a comprehensive, experiential piece that enabled students to put into practice what they learned in the classroom. We wanted the hotel to be profitable—a real-world enterprise in which students understood that a business must make money or it will fail.

We explored other university-owned hotels at Cornell University and the University of Delaware, both of which shared information generously. A steering committee of board members guided the process. Each trustee had experience that was useful: structuring financing, forming public-private partnerships, and dealing with government agencies.

A few Denver-based companies that owned and operated hotels throughout America and others familiar with university-owned facilities advised that the hotel needed a direct connection to the Hospitality Learning Center. Our plan was to create a wholly owned, nonprofit corporation that would own the hotel. Revenues from patrons would pay for the hotel and we would mount a capital campaign to pay for the attached learning center. The MSU Denver Foundation would raise $12 million, and the hotel's net profits would flow to the learning center to support scholarships.

Hotel labor would be supplied by our students. MSU Denver would structure an academic program to support the hotel's operation without "bright lines" between service and academics. The financial structure specified that the management company would receive a flat fee for its services, an unusual arrangement for hospitality operations and management.

A comprehensive RFP was designed to attract an organization that could bring all the elements together:

- Design and construction
- Management
- A flag, or name brand
- A financial package from the hotel chain

We received 10 bids, including several major hotel chains. The winning bid came from Sage Hospitality, a locally based hotel holding and management company. Sage operates hotels in Pittsburgh, Chicago, Minneapolis, Orlando, and Denver, including some Marriott properties. Marriott's SpringHill Suites was the flag they proposed, and Marriott offered the best financial package.

SpringHill Suites seemed like a good fit. It was a "select" rather than a full-service hotel. We didn't want to spend time and dollars on some of the extras required in a full-service hotel, like high-end decorations, room service, and bellmen. We added a quick-serve restaurant, partnering with the Denver-based Red Robin quick service chain.

Sage Hospitality's leadership made connecting the hotel and Hospitality Learning Center a bid condition. Just as we were about to embark on this huge project, the economy tanked. We had to decide whether to continue. By proceeding we would be able to take advantage of lower interest rates and construction costs. The risk was that MSU Denver might find itself with an empty hotel, a lingering recession, and unable to

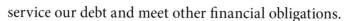

service our debt and meet other financial obligations.

Denver's economy hadn't suffered as badly as some other cities—Denver still had a good convention business. Our location on the edge of downtown—close to a football stadium, ballpark, and a sports arena for hockey and basketball promised healthy business—encouraged us to forge ahead, issuing bonds for the project in 2009.

The hotel opened in 2012 and within the first year our average occupancy was about 75 percent with more than a dozen sellout nights. Our room rate was $150 per night, $25 above the market forecast. Our goal is that 80 percent of the positions in the hotel be filled by our students. After graduating from the HTE program with experience at SpringHill Suites Denver Downtown, graduates will be qualified for management positions in other hotels.

The university's 2012–17 strategic plan ... adopted more innovative public-private partnerships and cross-functional collaborations that enabled programs to break out of rigid silos to resemble more real-world endeavors. The Franchise Ownership Program (was initiated because) Denver is one of America's major hubs for franchising, yet it has had no university-level training ground for franchise-owning entrepreneurs.

The original plan was to develop a franchising training program that would include a financing component so that someone completing the program would have access to funding and be matched with a franchise partner already vetted as a solid concept with a successful track record. Franchisors had been hurt by the recession and were struggling to recruit new franchisees due to the credit crunch.

The first financing model was a strict debt fund set up as a C-corporation that could accept both donations and private investors through the MSU Denver Foundation. Private investors would know upfront that their return would not be as high as in a regular venture fund. Our goal was to raise $2 million, but it rose to $25 million when a publicly-owned company in

Denver approached us about bringing institutional investors together and then managing the fund for a fee. The plan is to ramp the fund over time up to $100 million.

To participate, franchising companies must show they have at least 50 thriving locations and that a franchise applicant has the potential to generate enough revenue to pay him or herself a living wage. Program applicants—MSU Denver graduating seniors, alumni, and some community members—have to show they are a good credit risk and agree to make a 10 percent down payment—less than the SBA loan rules.

Students are able to get into a business for a relatively low cost while investors cut their risk by investing in well-established franchises that will be owned and run by people who have been trained by MSU Denver.

MSU Denver has also begun a Vendor Relationships Program through which vendors sign long-term lease agreements at market rates. Students and employees provide a built-in clientele. MSU Denver receives a percentage of gross sales that we funnel into our scholarship endowment as well as a cash gift from each business to endow a scholarship. As far as we know, we are the first university that has tried this concept.

We are constantly out in our community seeking opportunities that could spawn more public-private partnerships. One in its nascence is to build a program that takes advantage of Colorado's position as the second-largest aviation and aerospace cluster in America. Companies with bases here include Ball Aerospace, Lockheed Martin, United Launch Alliance, and Jeppesen.

City University of New York
By Charles A. Shorter, Trustee, and
Iris Weinshall, Vice Chancellor for Facility Planning,
Construction, and Management

In the fall of 2011, The City University of New York (CUNY) opened a gleaming $110 million building in the East Harlem neighborhood of Manhattan—a new home for The Lois V. and Samuel J. Silberman School of Social Work at Hunter College and CUNY School of Public Health at Hunter College. The new building, a satellite of Hunter College, was the result of a partnership between CUNY, the state, and three private entities—two philanthropic foundations and a major commercial developer.

Under normal circumstances, the project would have followed a typical process: CUNY would have needed to find a property, negotiate a price, bid out the construction, and pay for it all with a capital allocation from the State of New York. This project was the product of an arrangement that was intricate, imaginative, and instructive for CUNY by recognizing the value of our real estate portfolio. The opportunistic, rational use of land and buildings, whether owned or leased, is yielding new revenues and facilities.

CUNY has become more entrepreneurial, judiciously leveraging its substantial real estate assets. The largest urban public university in the country, CUNY has 24 campuses and 292 buildings. Nearly a third are individual properties on city streets, apart from a campus. The first step was to develop a comprehensive strategic plan for turning assets into new revenue.

CUNY's Office of Facilities Planning, Construction, and Management hired an independent construction firm with expertise in P3s. The firm identified five major university properties with leveraging opportunities totaling $390 million in potential revenues. The university pursued a number of recommendations, from selling and leasing some properties to redeveloping others in partnerships with private developers.

The creation of the new home for two of CUNY's most prominent professional schools started with a building in which CUNY was a tenant. The New York City Community Trust, which owned the building that housed the Hunter College School of Social Work, informed CUNY in 2007 that it planned to put the property on the market. The 10-story building on a residential street on Manhattan's Upper East Side had been the townhouse residence of prominent philanthropists Lois and Samuel Silberman. The family foundation donated the building to the Community Trust in 1969 and a few years later CUNY was given a 99-year, rent-free lease for its social work school.

Three decades later, the Community Trust stipulated that the university would receive approximately two-thirds of the proceeds of the sale to help relocate the social work school. But the university took it a step further, asking the trust to help find a new home for the School of Social Work that could also house CUNY's new School of Public Health. The trust agreed, bringing in a real estate firm to scout potential properties.

In the end, the New York City Trust agreed to sell the Silberman property to a private developer for $48 million, leveraging a long-term lease into $30 million in new capital funds. The state agreed to appropriate the additional $95 million needed to buy land and construct a new building in East Harlem that was larger and costlier than needed. With 24 campuses, there is never a shortage of needs. The CUNY Graduate Center had been in search of dormitory space for 15 years, so 100 units of graduate housing were added to the project.

The final piece of the puzzle was construction. CUNY negotiated a stipulation to the deal between the trust and the developer to acquire the former Silberman building on East 79th Street at the negotiated price. Brodsky had to construct the new building without receiving a management fee. Brodsky agreed, and put up the building in record time—14 months from groundbreaking—and about $20 million under budget.

The arrangement was so unusual for a public university system that the *New York Times* called the project "a multiparty real-estate deal of byzantine complexity." However, it was a success, proving that a public university can be as aggressive, successful, and entrepreneurial with its assets as some private institutions.

CUNY was drafting plans for a new community college when one of its six senior colleges, John Jay College of Criminal Justice, opened a new building on its campus on the West Side of Manhattan. That left vacant a building, once a shoe factory, on a large site in a prime location.

Building a new facility for a community college on its own would cost roughly $400 million. It would cost far less for the university to make use of something it already owned by partnering with a private developer to raze the existing building and construct a new, larger one that they could share. The property covers half of a city block, allowing for the development of up to 800,000 square feet of space.

Under the plan, CUNY will retain the lower half of a new building for its community college, while the developer would own roughly the top half and develop it as a mix of residential units and commercial space. Such a partnership would allow CUNY to finance a portion of the new college's facility with proceeds from the sale, without relying on the state for the full appropriation. The project is expected to draw significant interest from commercial developers.

Lessons learned: In 2007, the university engaged in a partnership with a leading developer in Brooklyn for a new building at its New York City College of Technology. The building was to be split between academic space for the college and commercial space for the developer, which would pay CUNY $48 million. But the deal fell apart over design issues and a dip in the real estate market that made the original plan less appealing to the developer.

Takeaways:

- Identify your goals upfront, set them out clearly, know your potential partners and whether they're a good match.
- Know what you have. Analyze your real estate holdings with a particular focus on location, to ascertain potential value.
- Look to the private sector to get the lay of the land. Meet with developers in your area—they're always on the lookout for a deal—to give you a sense of value and come up with varying development approaches.
- Have in place a fully developed, yet flexible, strategic real estate development plan that can provide a comprehensive road map for everyone involved, ensuring revenue generation and facility development that align with the institution's needs. Include predictable, steady flows of new income from a well-executed lease agreement or other real-estate transaction.
- Carefully plan the total approach for a transaction from start to finish. Anticipate the problems likely to be encountered in the development, including shifts in the real-estate market.
- Have your resources in place before undertaking any discussion or negotiation with the private sector.
- Exercise due diligence. Know who you're dealing with in any public-private partnership. Besides reputation and track record, understand your development partner's goals and needs.
- Employ full transparency. Keep the community fully informed and be conscious of its needs.

https://www.agb.org/trusteeship/2013/1/tale-2-cities-using-public-private-partnerships-create-higher-education-opportuni